Compassion

Compassion

A Reflection on the Christian Life

Text by
Donald P. McNeill
Douglas A. Morrison
Henri J. M. Nouwen

Drawings by
Joel Filártiga

DOUBLEDAY & COMPANY, INC.
GARDEN CITY, NEW YORK

Library of Congress Cataloging in Publication Data
McNeill, Donald.
Compassion, a reflection on the Christian life.
1. Sympathy.   2. Christianity and justice.
I. Morrison, Douglas.   II. Nouwen, Henri J. M.
III. Filártiga, Joel.   IV. Title.
BV4647.S9M38   248.4
AACR2
ISBN: 0-385-17699-6
Library of Congress Catalog Card Number: 81-65660

If our life in Christ means anything to you, if love can per-suade at all, or the Spirit that we have in common, or any tenderness and sympathy, then be united in your convic-tions and united in your love, with a common purpose and a common mind. That is the one thing which would make me completely happy. There must be no competition among you, no conceit; but everybody is to be self-effacing. Always consider the other person to be better than yourself, so that nobody thinks of his own interests first but everybody thinks of other people's interests instead. In your minds you must be the same as Christ Jesus:

> *His state was divine,*
> *yet he did not cling*
> *to his equality with God*
> *but emptied himself*
> *to assume the condition of a slave,*
> *and became as we are;*
> *and being as we are,*
> *he was humbler yet,*
> *even to accepting death,*
> *death on a cross.*
> *But God raised him high*
> *and gave him the name*
> *which is above all other names*
> *so that all beings*
> *in the heavens, on earth and in the underworld,*
> *should bend the knee at the name of Jesus*
> *and that every tongue should acclaim*
> *Jesus Christ as Lord,*
> *to the glory of God the Father.*

(Ph 2:6–11)

Contents

PREFACE   xi

ACKNOWLEDGMENTS   xiii

INTRODUCTION   1

PART ONE: THE COMPASSIONATE GOD   11

  1   God-with-Us   13
  2   Servant God   23
  3   Obedient God   34

PART TWO: THE COMPASSIONATE LIFE   47

  4   Community   49
  5   Displacement   62
  6   Togetherness   75

PART THREE: THE COMPASSIONATE WAY   87

  7   Patience   89
  8   Prayer   103
  9   Action   116

CONCLUSION   131

EPILOGUE   137

NOTES   143

Preface

This book began in a small Greek restaurant in Washington, D.C. As we sat in the empty subterranean dining room expressing our discontent with the individualism and spiritual dryness of our academic lives at Notre Dame, Catholic University, and Yale, the three of us found ourselves scribbling notes on our table napkins. This time, unlike many others, our complaints led not to idleness but to a plan to meet on nine Thursdays in the capital city to study and pray together. Being teachers of pastoral theology and finding ourselves in the city where great political power is sought, acquired, and exercised, the question of how to live compassionately in our world presented itself as the most urgent question for our meetings.

These reflections on compassion have emerged from those nine Thursday meetings. The first formulations of what compassion might mean in our society were born in dialogue with those whom we had occasionally invited to join our discussions: Walter Burkhardt, S.J., theologian and member of the faculty of Catholic University; Parker Palmer, sociologist of religion and Dean of Studies at the Quaker community, Pendle Hill; Mike Heissler, medical student at George Washington University; Patrick Leahy, U. S. Senator from Vermont, and his wife, Marcelle; the late Hubert Humphrey, U. S. Senator from Minnesota; Betty Carroll and Carol Coston, religious sisters working with the Center of Concern and with Network; Jim Wallis and Wes Michaelson, editors of *Sojourners;* and the Little Sisters of Jesus, who live, work, and pray as contemplatives in the midst of Washington, D.C. They all shared considerable time with us and offered us numerous ideas, suggestions, and experiences that became the rich soil from which this book grew.

Quite a few years have passed since the conclusion of those meetings. They were years of testing, reformulating, and reevaluating many of our original thoughts. Now that we feel confident enough to put our reflections in print, we want to express our sincere thanks to these "early pioneers" without whom this book would never have been written. Just as the pioneers of this country would find it difficult to recognize today the country they explored, so our friends may have a difficult time discerning in these pages the insights they offered. But those insights are here, and form the backbone of this book.

We also want to express our deep gratitude to the Paraguayan doctor Joel Filártiga. His powerful illustrations, born from the tragedy in his own life, add to this book a dimension that far exceeds both our experiences and our words. The story of Joel, which we tell in the Epilogue, explains why his drawings have become an integral part of this book.

Acknowledgments

Although we planned this book as the work of three friends, the final text is the result of suggestions, comments, criticisms, and contributions of many people who encouraged us in our work together.

We want to thank all those who helped us in the rewriting of the manuscript by critically reading it or by using it in their teaching. They are: Bob Antonelli, Judith Anne Beattie, Jane Bouvier, Steven Cribari, Agnes McNeill Donohue, James Duane, James Fee, George Fitzgerald, Stacy Hennessy, George Hunsinger, Ben Hunt, Ken and Penny Jameson, Mark Janus, Jay Kenney, Carol Knoll, Mary Meg McCarthy, Kay and Don McNeill, Melanie Morrison, Claude Pomerleau, John Roark, Jim and Mary Ann Roemer, Louis ter Steeg, Naomi Burton Stone, Reg and Ralph Weissert, Vivian Whitehead, Colin Williams, and Gregory Youngchild.

We also want to express our gratitude to Piet van Leeuwen and Mark Fedor for their secretarial assistance; and to Robert Moore, Joseph Núñez, Richard Schaper, and Mich Zeman for their editorial collaboration during the final phases of this book.

To Robert Heller of Doubleday we offer our thanks for his patience and encouragement during the last five years.

Finally, a special word of gratitude goes to John Mogabgab, who not only coordinated much of our work on this book but also made essential contributions to its content and form.

DONALD MCNEILL
DOUGLAS MORRISON
HENRI NOUWEN

Introduction

The word *compassion* generally evokes positive feelings. We like to think of ourselves as compassionate people who are basically good, gentle, and understanding. We more or less assume that compassion is a natural response to human suffering. Who would not feel compassion for a poor old man, a hungry child, a paralyzed soldier, a fearful girl? It seems almost impossible to imagine that compassion does not belong among our most self-evident human qualities. Do we not feel deeply offended when someone accuses us of lacking compassion? Does that not sound as if we are accused of a lack of humanity? Indeed, we immediately identify being compassionate with being human. An incompassionate human being seems as inconceivable as a nonhuman human being.

But, if being human and being compassionate are the same,

then why is humanity torn by conflict, war, hatred, and oppression? Why, then, are there so many people in our midst who suffer from hunger, cold, and lack of shelter? Why, then, do differences in race, sex, or religion prevent us from approaching each other and forming community? Why, then, are millions of human beings suffering from alienation, separation, or loneliness? Why, then, do we hurt, torture, and kill each other? Why, then, is our world in such chaos?

Questions such as these suggest that we need to take a critical look at our understanding of compassion. The word *compassion* is derived from the Latin words *pati* and *cum*, which together mean "to suffer with." Compassion asks us to go where it hurts, to enter into places of pain, to share in brokenness, fear, confusion, and anguish. Compassion challenges us to cry out with those in misery, to mourn with those who are lonely, to weep with those in tears. Compassion requires us to be weak with the weak, vulnerable with the vulnerable, and powerless with the powerless. Compassion means full immersion in the condition of being human. When we look at compassion this way, it becomes clear that something more is involved than a general kindness or tenderheartedness. It is not surprising that compassion, understood as suffering with, often evokes in us a deep resistance and even protest. We are inclined to say, "This is self-flagellation, this is masochism, this is a morbid interest in pain, this is a sick desire." It is important for us to acknowledge this resistance and to recognize that suffering is not something we desire or to which we are attracted. On the contrary, it is something we want to avoid at all cost. Therefore, compassion is not among our most natural responses. We are pain-avoiders and we consider anyone who feels attracted to suffering abnormal, or at least very unusual.

Compassion thus is not as natural a phenomenon as it might first appear. We should therefore not be surprised to find some people say without hesitation that a compassionate society is a sick society. Peregrine Worsthorne expresses this "incompassionate" point of view when he writes:

A genuine compassionate society, one that has succeeded in achieving the ideal of actually putting itself in the shoes of the unfortunate, will soon find itself marching in the direction of collective solutions inimical to individual freedom. . . . There is a real and awful danger of people actually beginning to identify with the world of suffering. . . . No healthy society should allow itself to see the world through the eyes of the unfortunate, since the unfortunate have no great interest in perceiving, let alone exploiting, the highest value of civilization: individual freedom. Indeed, being for the most part those who have failed to make use of freedom, either because of fate or circumstances . . . they are likely to be the part of society least enamored of that supremely challenging ideal and most susceptible to all the temptations to undermine it.[1]

These words probably seem very harsh, but they may be more representative of our way of living and acting than we are ready to confess. Although we might not be as eager as Peregrine Worsthorne to reject compassion in the name of individual freedom, it is not unlikely that in fact we are close to his basic conviction that compassion cannot and should not constitute the core of human motivation. If we give compassion a place at all in our daily concerns, we consider such a place at best to be on the periphery of our thoughts and actions. Like Peregrine Worsthorne, we too are skeptical about a world governed by compassion. The idea of such a world strikes us as naïve, romantic, or at least unrealistic. We "know" too well that our civilization will not survive if the crucial decisions are in the hands of truly compassionate people. For those who do not live in a dream world and keep their eyes open to the facts of life, compassion can at most be a small and subservient part of our competitive existence.

This sobering idea was forcefully brought home to us during

the early stages of this book. One day, the three of us visited the late Senator Hubert Humphrey to ask him about compassion in politics. We had come because we felt he was one of the most caring human beings in the political arena. The Senator, who had just finished talking with the ambassador of Bangladesh and obviously expected a complaint, a demand, or a compliment, was visibly caught off guard when asked how he felt about compassion in politics. Instinctively, he left his large mahogany desk, over which hung the emblem reminding visitors that they were speaking with the former Vice-President of the United States, and joined us around a small coffee table. But then, after having adapted himself to the somewhat unusual situation, Senator Humphrey walked back to his desk, picked up a long pencil with a small eraser at its end, and said in his famous high-pitched voice: "Gentlemen, look at this pencil. Just as the eraser is only a very small part of this pencil and is used only when you make a mistake, so compassion is only called upon when things get out of hand. The main part of life is competition; only the eraser is compassion. It is sad to say, gentlemen, but in politics compassion is just part of the competition."

Compassion erases the mistakes of life, just as the rubber end of a pencil removes the smudges on the paper. Perhaps this is how most of us really feel and think when we are honest with ourselves. Compassion is neither our central concern nor our primary stance in life. What we really desire is to make it in life, to get ahead, to be first, to be different. We want to forge our identities by carving out for ourselves niches in life where we can maintain a safe distance from others. We do not aspire to suffer with others. On the contrary, we develop methods and techniques that allow us to stay away from pain. Hospitals and funeral homes often become places to hide the sick and the dead. Suffering is unattractive, if not repelling and disgusting. The less we are confronted with it, the better. This is our principal attitude, and in this context compassion means no more than the small soft eraser at the end of a long hard pencil. To be compassionate then means to be kind and gentle to those who get hurt by competition. A miner who gets caught underground evokes compassion; a student who breaks down under the pressure of exams evokes compassion; a mother on welfare who does not have enough food and clothes for her children evokes compassion; an elderly woman who is dying alone in the anonymity of a big city evokes compassion. But our primary frame of reference remains competition. After all, we need coal and intellectuals, and all systems have their shortcomings!

Thus, what at first seemed to be such a natural human virtue proves to be much less so than we thought. Where does this leave us? Well, it is precisely this ambiguous place of compassion in our lives that provides both the reason for this book and its starting point. Must we simply recognize that we are more competitive than compassionate, and try to make the best of it with a "healthy dose of skepticism"? Is the best advice we can give each other that we should try to live in such a way that we hurt each other as little as possible? Is our greatest ideal a maximum of satisfaction with a minimum of pain?

This book says *No* to these questions, and proposes that in order to understand the place of compassion in our lives, we must look in a radically different direction. The perspective presented here is based on the words of Jesus, "Be compassionate as your Father is compassionate" (Lk 6:36), and is offered in the deep conviction that through compassion our humanity grows into its fullness. This is not said lightly. It is said after years of discussing, reading, writing, and many—often painful—experiences. There have been moments during which we were tempted to drop this project and move to easier subjects. But each time we faced this temptation, we realized that we were doubting the value of a commitment to Christ. As the call to compassion slowly revealed itself to us as the center of Christian life, the thought of ignoring this call—even in writing—increasingly appeared to be a refusal to face directly the radical challenge of our faith.

In the first phase of our work together, we discussed the life, work, and deeds of Jesus Christ on the assumption that all people have a natural desire to be compassionate. Since those days, however, we have become less optimistic and, hopefully, more realistic. National and international events, deeper study of the Scriptures, and the many critical responses of friends, have made us less confident about our "compassionate tendencies" and more aware of the radical quality of Jesus' command: "Be compassionate as your Father is compassionate." This command does not restate the obvious, something we already wanted but had forgotten, an idea in line with our natural aspirations. On the contrary, it is a call that goes right against the grain; that turns us completely around and requires a total conversion of heart and mind. It is indeed a radical call, a call that goes to the roots of our lives.

This increasing awareness of the radical nature of Christ's call to compassion has determined the organization of this book. We want to speak, first of all, about the compassionate God who is revealed to us in Jesus Christ, because God's own compassion constitutes the basis and source of our compassion. Secondly, we want to explore what it means to live a compassionate life as followers of Christ, for it is only in discipleship that we can begin to understand the call to be compassionate as the Father is compassionate. Finally, we want to discuss the compassionate way of prayer and action because it is through these disciplines, which guide our relationships with God and our fellow human beings, that God's compassion can manifest itself. If those who read this book—whatever their particular vocation in life may be—feel deepened in their awareness of the presence of a compassionate God in the midst of an incompassionate world, we will have ample reason for gratitude.

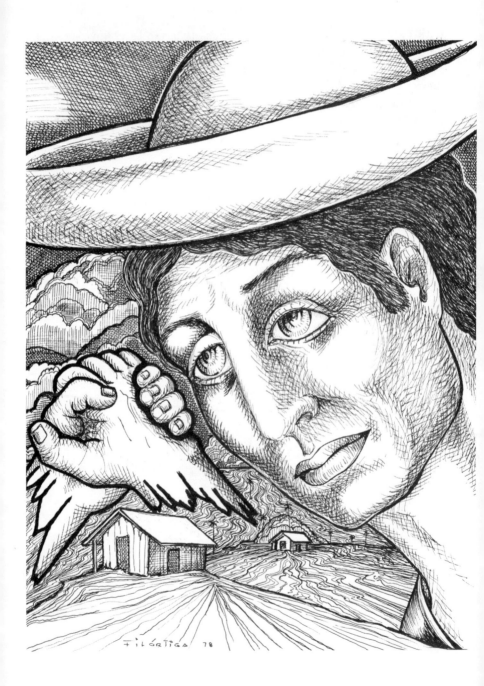

PART ONE

The Compassionate God

1

God-with-Us

IN SOLIDARITY

God is a compassionate God. This means, first of all, that he is a God who has chosen to be God-with-us. To be able to know and feel better this divine solidarity, let us explore the experience of someone being truly with us.

When do we receive real comfort and consolation? Is it when someone teaches us how to think or act? Is it when we receive advice about where to go or what to do? Is it when we hear words of reassurance and hope? Sometimes, perhaps. But what really counts is that in moments of pain and suffering someone stays with us. More important than any particular action or word of advice is the simple presence of someone who cares. When someone says to us in the midst of a crisis, "I do not know what to say or what to do, but I want you to realize that I am with you, that I will not leave you alone," we have a friend through whom we can find consolation and comfort. In a time so filled with methods and techniques designed to change people, to influence their behavior, and to make them do new things and think new thoughts, we have lost the simple but difficult gift of being present to each other. We have lost this gift because we have been led to believe that presence must be useful. We say, "Why should I visit this person? I can't do anything anyway. I don't even have anything to say. Of what use can I be?" Meanwhile, we have forgotten that it is often in "useless," unpretentious, humble presence to each other that we feel consolation and comfort. Simply being with someone is difficult because it asks of us that we share in the other's vulnerability, enter with him or her into the experience of weakness and powerlessness, become part of uncertainty, and give up control and self-determination. And still, whenever this happens, new strength and new hope is being born. Those who offer us comfort and consolation by being and staying with us in moments of illness, mental anguish, or spiritual darkness often grow as close to us as those with whom we have biological ties. They show their solidarity with us by willingly entering the dark, uncharted spaces of our lives. For this reason, they are the ones who bring new hope and help us discover new directions.

These reflections offer only a glimpse of what we mean when we say that God is a God-with-us, a God who came to share our lives in solidarity. It does not mean that God solves our problems, shows us the way out of our confusion, or offers answers for our many questions. He might do all of that, but his solidarity consists in the fact that he is willing to enter with us into our problems, confusions, and questions.

That is the good news of God's taking on human flesh. The Evangelist Matthew, after describing the birth of Jesus, writes: "Now all this took place to fulfil the words spoken by the Lord through the prophet: 'The Virgin shall conceive and give birth to a son and they will call him Immanuel,' a name which means 'God-is-with-us' " (Mt 1:22–23).

As soon as we call God, "God-with-us," we enter into a new relationship of intimacy with him. By calling him Immanuel, we recognize that he has committed himself to live in solidarity with us, to share our joys and pains, to defend and protect us, and to suffer all of life with us. The God-with-us is a close God, a God whom we call our refuge, our stronghold, our wisdom, and even, more intimately, our helper, our shepherd, our love. We will never really know God as a compassionate God if we do not understand with our heart and mind that "he lived among us" (Jn 1:14).

Often we say to each other in a bitter tone: "You do not know what you are talking about because you did not march in protest, participate in the strike, or experience the hatred of the bystanders, because you were never hungry, never knew cold, or never felt real isolation." When we say such things, we express the deep conviction that we are willing to listen to consoling words only when they are born out of solidarity with the condition that was or is ours. God wants to know our condition fully and does not want to take away any pain which he himself has not fully tasted. His compassion is anchored in the most intimate solidarity, a solidarity that allows us to say with the psalmist, "This is our God, and we are the people he pastures, the flock that he guides" (Ps 95:7).

WITH GUT FEELINGS

How do we know this is anything more than a beautiful idea? How do we know that God is our God and not a stranger, an outsider, a passerby?

We know this because in Jesus, God's compassion became visible to us. Jesus not only said, "Be compassionate as your

Father is compassionate," but he also was the concrete embodiment of this divine compassion in our world. Jesus' response to the ignorant, the hungry, the blind, the lepers, the widows, and all those who came to him with their suffering, flowed from the divine compassion which led God to become one of us. We need to pay close attention to Jesus' words and actions if we are to gain insight into the mystery of this divine compassion. We would misunderstand the many miraculous stories in the Gospels if we were to be impressed simply by the fact that sick and tormented people were suddenly liberated from their pains. If this were indeed the central event of these stories, a cynic might rightly remark that most people during Jesus' day were *not* cured and that those who were cured only made it worse for those who were not. What is important here is not the cure of the sick, but the deep compassion that moved Jesus to these cures.

There is a beautiful expression in the Gospels that appears only twelve times and is used exclusively in reference to Jesus or his Father. That expression is "to be moved with compassion." The Greek verb *splangchnizomai* reveals to us the deep and powerful meaning of this expression. The *splangchna* are the entrails of the body, or as we might say today, the guts. They are the place where our most intimate and intense emotions are located. They are the center from which both passionate love and passionate hate grow. When the Gospels speak about Jesus' compassion as his being moved in the entrails, they are expressing something very deep and mysterious. The compassion that Jesus felt was obviously quite different from superficial or passing feelings of sorrow or sympathy. Rather, it extended to the most vulnerable part of his being. It is related to the Hebrew word for compassion, *rachamim*, which refers to the womb of Yahweh. Indeed, compassion is such a deep, central, and powerful emotion in Jesus that it can only be described as a movement of the womb of God. There, all the divine tenderness and gentleness lies hidden. There, God is father and mother, brother and sister, son and daughter. There, all feelings, emotions, and passions are one in divine love. When Jesus was moved to compassion, the source of all life trembled, the ground of all love burst open, and the abyss of God's immense, inexhaustible, and unfathomable tenderness revealed itself.

This is the mystery of God's compassion as it becomes visible in the healing stories of the New Testament. When Jesus saw the crowd harassed and dejected like sheep without a shepherd, he felt with them in the center of his being (Mt 9:36). When he saw the blind, the paralyzed, and the deaf being brought to him from all directions, he trembled from within and experienced their pains in his own heart (Mt 14:14). When he noticed that the thousands who had followed him for days were tired and hungry, he said, I am moved with compassion (Mk 8:2). And so it was with the two blind men who called after him (Mt 9:27), the leper who fell to his knees in front of him (Mk 1:41), and the widow of Nain who was burying her only son (Lk 7:13). They moved him, they made him feel with all his intimate sensibilities the depth of their sorrow. He became lost with the lost, hungry with the hungry, and sick with the sick. In him, all suffering was sensed with a perfect sensitivity. The great mystery revealed to us in this is that Jesus, who is the sinless son of God, chose in total freedom to suffer fully our pains and thus to let us discover the true nature of our own passions. In him, we see and experience the persons we truly are. He who is divine lives our broken humanity not as a curse (Gn 3:14–19), but as a blessing. His divine compassion makes it possible for us to face our sinful selves, because it transforms our broken human condition from a cause of despair into a source of hope.

This is what we mean when we say that Jesus Christ reveals God's solidarity with us. In and through Jesus Christ we know that God is our God, a God who has experienced our brokenness, who has become sin for us (2 Co 5:21). He has embraced everything human with the infinite tenderness of his compassion.

TOWARD NEW LIFE

But what about the cures? Did not the blind see, the lepers become pure, the paralyzed walk again, and the widow see her son come back to life? Is that not what counts? Is that not what proves that God is God and he really loves us? Let us be very careful with our pragmatism. It was out of his compassion that Jesus' healing emerged. He did not cure to prove, to impress, or to convince. His cures were the natural expression of his being our God. The mystery of God's love is not that he takes our pains away, but that he first wants to share them with us. Out of this divine solidarity comes new life. Jesus' being moved in the center of his being by human pain is indeed a movement toward new life. God is our God, the God of the living. In his divine womb life is always born again. The great mystery is not the cures, but the infinite compassion which is their source.

We know too well what it means when cures are performed without compassion. We have seen men and women who can walk again, see again, speak again, but whose hearts remain dark and bitter. We know too well that cures not born out of care are false cures leading not to light but to darkness. Let us not fool ourselves with a shortcut to new life. The many cures by Jesus recorded in the Gospels can never be separated from his being with us. They witness to the infinite fecundity of his divine compassion, and show us the beautiful fruits of his solidarity with our condition. The truly good news is that God is not a distant God, a God to be feared and avoided, a God of revenge, but a God who is moved by our pains and participates in the fullness of the human struggle. The miraculous cures in the Gospels are hopeful and joyful reminders of this good news, which is our true consolation and comfort.

OUR COMPETITIVE SELVES

When we take a critical look at ourselves, we have to recognize that competition, not compassion, is our main motivation in life. We find ourselves deeply immersed in all sorts of competition. Our whole sense of self is dependent upon the way we compare ourselves with others and upon the differences we can identify. When the question "Who am I?" is put to the powers of this world—school officials, church representatives, placement officers, athletic directors, factory managers, television and radio announcers—the answer is simply, "You are the difference you make." It is by our differences, distinctions, that we are recognized, honored, rejected, or despised. Whether we are more or less intelligent, practical, strong, fast, handy, or handsome depends upon those with whom we are compared or those with whom we compete. It is upon these positive or negative distinctions that much of our self-esteem depends. It does not take much reflection to realize that in all family problems, race conflicts, class confrontations, and national or international disputes, these real or imaginary distinctions play a central role. Indeed, we invest much of our energy in defending the differences between people and groups of people. Thus, we define ourselves in ways that require us to maintain distance from one another. We are very protective of our "trophies." After all, who are we if we cannot proudly point to something special that sets us apart from others?

This all-pervasive competition, which reaches into the smallest corners of our relationships, prevents us from entering into full solidarity with each other, and stands in the way of our being compassionate. We prefer to keep compassion on the periphery of our competitive lives. Being compassionate would require giving up dividing lines and relinquishing differences and distinctions. And that would mean losing our identities! This makes it clear why the call to be compassionate is so frightening and evokes such deep resistance.

This fear, which is very real and influences much of our behavior, betrays our deepest illusions: that we can forge our own identities; that we are the collective impressions of our surroundings; that we are the trophies and distinctions we have won. This, indeed, is our greatest illusion. It makes us into competitive people who compulsively cling to our differences and defend them at all cost, even to the point of violence.

A NEW SELF

The compassion Jesus offers challenges us to give up our fearful clinging and to enter with him into the fearless life of God himself. In saying, "Be compassionate as your Father is compassionate," Jesus invites us to be as close to each other as God is to us. He even asks us to love one another with God's own compassion. A divine compassion is a compassion without the slightest tinge of competition. Therefore, only God can be wholly compassionate because only he is not in competition with us. The paradox of God's compassion is that God can be compassionate because he is God; that is, wholly other than we are. Because God is wholly other, he can become wholly as we are. He can become so deeply human because he is so fully divine. In short, God can be fully compassionate because he does not compare himself with us and thus is in no way in competition with us.

Jesus' command, "Be compassionate as your Father is compassionate," is a command to participate in the compassion of God himself. He requires us to unmask the illusion of our competitive selfhood, to give up clinging to our imaginary distinctions as sources of identity, and to be taken up into the same intimacy with God which he himself knows. This is the mystery of the Christian life: to receive a new self, a new identity, which depends not on what we can achieve, but on

what we are willing to receive. This new self is our participation in the divine life in and through Christ. Jesus wants us
to belong to God as he belongs to God; he wants us to be
children of God as he is a child of God; he wants us to let go
of the old life, which is so full of fears and doubts, and to receive the new life, the life of God himself. In and through
Christ we receive a new identity that enables us to say, "I am
not the esteem I can collect through competition, but the
love I have freely received from God." It allows us to say
with Paul, "I live now not with my own life but with the life
of Christ who lives in me" (Ga 2:20).

This new self, the self of Jesus Christ, makes it possible for
us to be compassionate as our Father is compassionate.
Through union with him, we are lifted out of our competitiveness with each other into the divine wholeness. By sharing
in the wholeness of the one in whom no competition exists,
we can enter into new, compassionate relationships with each
other. By accepting our identities from the one who is the
giver of all life, we can be with each other without
distance or fear. This new identity, free from greed and
desire for power, allows us to enter so fully and uncondi-
tionally into the sufferings of others that it becomes
possible for us to heal the sick and call the dead to life. When
we share in God's compassion, a whole new way of living
opens itself to us, a way of living we glimpse in the lives of
the Apostles and those great Christians who have witnessed
for Christ through the centuries. This divine compassion is
not, like our self-made compassion, part of the competition.
Rather, it is the expression of a new way of living in which
interpersonal comparisons, rivalries, and competitions are
gradually left behind.

Paul gives us a beautiful example of this new-found compassion in his letter to the Philippians. There he writes: God
is my witness how much I miss you all with the tender compassion [the *splangchna*] of Christ Jesus (Ph 1:8). Paul feels
for his people with the same divine intensity that Jesus felt

for those who came to him with their pain. The mystery is that Paul loves his people with a divine intimacy. His compassion is thus much more than mere sympathy or emotional attachment. It is the expression of his new being in Christ. In Christ, Paul has become capable of the all-embracing and deeply moving compassion of God. He therefore says, "I miss you in the *splangchna* of Christ," that is, with Christ's own most intimate divine interiority. Paul's new life in Christ, through which he was lifted above rivalry and competition, allowed him to extend divine compassion to his people. This reveals to us the great mystery of Paul's ministry. He touched people with God's compassion, a compassion so deep and so full that it could not fail to bear fruit. This also is the mystery of our new way of being together. It has become possible to be together in compassion because we have been given a share in God's compassion. In and through this compassion, we can begin to live in solidarity with each other as fully and intimately as God lives with us.

2

Servant God

HE EMPTIED HIMSELF

God's compassion is not something abstract or indefinite, but a concrete, specific gesture in which God reaches out to us. In Jesus Christ we see the fullness of God's compassion. To us, who cry out from the depth of our brokenness for a hand that will touch us, an arm that can embrace us, lips that will kiss us, a word that speaks to us here and now, and a heart that is not afraid of our fears and tremblings; to us, who feel our own pain as no other human being feels it, has felt it, or ever will feel it and who are always waiting for someone who dares to come close—to us a man has come who could truly say, "I am with you." Jesus Christ, who is God-with-us, has come to us in the freedom of love, not needing to experience our human condition but freely choosing to do so out of love.

This mystery of God-with-us in Jesus Christ cannot be grasped. But we can and must enter it humbly and reverently to find there the source of our comfort and consolation. When Jesus was no longer with his disciples, new words were found by the early Christian community to express the mystery of God's compassion. Among the most beautiful and profound of these expressions is the Hymn of Christ which Paul uses in his letter to the Philippians:

> His state was divine,
> yet he did not cling
> to his equality with God
> but emptied himself
> to assume the condition of a slave,
> and became as we are;
> and being as we are,
> he was humbler yet,
> even to accepting death,
> death on a cross.

> (Ph 2:6–8)

Here we see that the compassionate God who revealed himself to us in Jesus Christ is the God who became a servant. Our God is a servant God. It is difficult for us to comprehend that we are liberated by someone who became powerless, that we are being strengthened by someone who became weak, that we find new hope in someone who divested himself of all distinctions, and that we find a leader in someone who became a servant. It is beyond our intellectual and emotional grasp. We expect freedom from someone who is not as imprisoned as we are, health from someone who is not as sick as we are, and new directions from someone who is not as lost and confused as we are.

But of Jesus it is said that he emptied himself and assumed the condition of a slave. To be a slave means to be subject not only to human but also to superhuman powers. It is the condition of powerlessness in which one feels victimized by uncontrollable events, anonymous influences, and capricious agents which surround and elude one's understanding and control. In the culture in which the Gospel was first proclaimed, these powers were often perceived as antagonistic and cruel gods. In our day these powers are no longer personalized, but they remain very real and no less fearful. Nuclear warheads and power plants, millions of hungry and dying people, torture chambers and immense cruelties, the increase in robberies, rapes, and twisted, sadistic plots, all give us the feeling of being surrounded by a mysterious network of powers that can destroy us any day or hour. The awareness that we have hardly any influence on our own way of living and working, and the realization that at any moment something could happen that could permanently destroy our life, health, or happiness, can fill us with an all-pervading sadness and fear.

Is it surprising that, this being our condition, we look away from our frightening surroundings, away from the here and now, to something and someone "above" for liberation from this slavery? In Jesus' day, as well as ours, we find an intense desire for something unusual, abnormal, and spectacular that can pull us up out of our misery into a sphere where we are at a safe distance from the world that threatens to swallow us.

HE WAS HUMBLER YET

But it is not said of Jesus that he reached down from on high to pull us up from slavery, but that he became a slave with us. God's compassion is a compassion that reveals itself in servanthood. Jesus became subject to the same powers and influences that dominate us, and suffered our fears, uncertainties, and anxieties with us. Jesus emptied himself. He gave up a privileged position, a position of majesty and power, and assumed fully and without reservation a condition of total dependency. Paul's hymn of Christ does not ask us to look upward, away from our condition, but to look in our midst and discover God there.

This is not the last word, however. "Being as we are, he was humbler yet, even to accepting death, death on a cross." Here the essence of God's compassion is announced. Not only did he taste fully the dependent and fearful condition of being human, but he also experienced the most despicable, and horrifying form of death—death on a cross. Not only did he become human, but he also became human in the most dejected and rejected way. Not only did he know human uncertainties and fears, but he also experienced the agony, pain, and total degradation of the bloody torture and death of a convicted criminal. In this humiliation, Jesus lived out the full implications of emptying himself to be with us in compassion. He not only suffered our painful human condition in all its concreteness but he also suffered death with us in one of its rawest, ugliest, and most degrading forms. It was a death that we "normal" human beings would hardly be willing to consider ours.

In the Gospel stories of Jesus' healings, we sense how close God wants to be with those who suffer. But now we see the price God is willing to pay for this intimacy. It is the price of ultimate servanthood, the price of becoming a slave, completely dependent on strange, cruel, alien forces. We spontaneously protest against this road of self-emptying and humiliation. We certainly appreciate people who try to understand us. We are even grateful for those who want to feel with us. But we become suspicious when someone chooses to undergo the pain that we would avoid at all costs. We understand conditional solidarity, but we do not understand solidarity that has no limits.

THE DOWNWARD PULL

Jesus' compassion is characterized by a downward pull. That is what disturbs us. We cannot even think about ourselves in terms other than those of an upward pull, an upward mobility in which we strive for better lives, higher salaries, and more prestigious positions. Thus, we are deeply disturbed by a God who embodies a downward movement. Instead of striving for a higher position, more power, and more influence, Jesus moves, as Karl Barth says, from "the heights to the depth, from victory to defeat, from riches to poverty, from triumph to suffering, from life to death."[2] Jesus' whole life and mission involve accepting powerlessness and revealing in this powerlessness the limitlessness of God's love. Here we see what compassion means. It is not a bending toward the underprivileged from a privileged position; it is not a reaching out from on high to those who are less fortunate below; it is not a gesture of sympathy or pity for those who fail to make it in the upward pull. On the contrary, compassion means going directly to those people and places where suffering is most acute and building a home there. God's compassion is total, absolute, unconditional, without reservation. It is the compassion of the one who keeps going to the most forgotten corners of the world, and who cannot rest as long as he knows that there are still human beings with tears in their eyes. It is the compassion of a God who does not merely act as a servant, but whose servanthood is a direct expression of his divinity.

The hymn of Christ makes us see that God reveals his divine love for us in his coming to us as a servant. The great mystery of God's compassion is that in his compassion, in his entering with us into the condition of a slave, he reveals himself to us as God. His becoming a servant is not an exception to his being God. His self-emptying and humiliation are not a step away from his true nature. His becoming as we are and dying on a cross is not a temporary interruption of his own divine existence. Rather, in the emptied and humbled Christ we encounter God, we see who God really is, we come to know his true divinity. Precisely because God is God, he can reveal his divinity in the form of a servant. As Karl Barth says, "God does not have to dishonor himself, when he goes into the far country and conceals his glory. For he is truly honored in his concealment. This concealment, and therefore his condescension as such, is the image and the reflection in which we see him as he is."[3] In his servanthood God does not disfigure himself, he does not take on something alien to himself, he does not act against or in spite of his divine self. On the contrary, it is in his servanthood that God chooses to reveal himself as God to us. Therefore, we can say that the downward pull as we see this in Jesus Christ is not a movement away from God, but a movement toward him as he really is: A God for us who came not to rule but to serve. This implies very specifically that God does not want to be known except through servanthood and that, therefore, servanthood is God's self-revelation.

IN HIS PATH

Here a new dimension of our call to compassion becomes apparent. If God's compassion reveals itself in the downward path of Jesus Christ, then our compassion toward each other will involve following in his path and participating in this self-emptying, humiliating movement. There is little doubt that the disciples of Jesus understood their call as a call to make God's compassion present in this world by moving with Jesus into positions of servanthood. Peter writes, "Wrap yourselves in humility to be servants of each other" (1 P 5:5). He thus echoes the many invitations of Jesus to follow him on his humbling way: "The one who humbles himself will be exalted" (Lk 14:11). "Anyone who loses his life for my sake, and for the sake of the gospel, will save it" (Mk 8:35). "The one who makes himself as little as this little child is the greatest in the kingdom of heaven" (Mt 18:4). "If anyone wants to be a follower of mine, let him renounce himself and take up his cross and follow me" (Mk 8:34). "How happy are the poor in spirit . . . those who mourn . . . those who hunger . . . who are persecuted" (Mt 5:3–10). "Love your enemies and pray for those who persecute you" (Mt 5:44).

This is the way of Jesus and the way to which he calls his disciples. It is the way that at first frightens or at least embarrasses us. Who wants to be humble? Who wants to be the last? Who wants to be like a little, powerless child? Who desires to lose his or her life, to be poor, mourning, and hungry? All this appears to be against our natural inclinations. But once we see that Jesus reveals to us, in his radically downward pull, the compassionate nature of God, we begin to understand that to follow him is to participate in the ongoing self-revelation of God. By setting out with Jesus on the road of the cross, we become people in whose lives the compassionate presence of God in this world can manifest itself. As Barth observes, what seemed to be unnatural from the perspective of the world becomes natural for the follower of Christ.[4] Just as in Christ's servanthood God's nature becomes evident, so for those who want to proclaim God's presence in the world, servanthood becomes a natural response. Thus, Paul could say to the Colossians, "It makes me happy to suffer for you, as I am suffering now, and in my own body to do what I can to make up all that has still to be undergone by Christ for the sake of his body, the Church" (Col 1:24). For Paul, servanthood had become natural. It belonged to his new being in Christ.

OUR SECOND NATURE

Our "second nature," the nature we receive in and through Christ, sets us free to live compassionately in servanthood.

Compassion is no longer a virtue that we must exercise in special circumstances or an attitude that we must call upon when other ways of responding have been exhausted, but it is the *natural* way of being in the world. This "second nature" also allows us to see compassion not in moralistic terms, that is, in terms of how we have to behave as good Christians, but as a new way of being in the world. As Christians, we are called to be ambassadors of Christ in whom the reality of God's infinite compassion becomes concrete and tangible (2 Co 5:20). To become humble servants with Christ in discipleship is to become witnesses of the living God. The Christian life is a life of witnessing through servanthood to the compassionate God, not a life in which we seek suffering and pain.

To the outsider, much Christian behavior seems to be naïve, impractical, and often little less than an exercise in self-flagellation. The outsider understandably believes that anyone who feels attracted to suffering and pain and who desires to humble himself or herself to a position of servanthood cannot be taken very seriously. Striving to be a slave seems such a perverted way of living that it offends human sensibilities. Nobody finds anything wrong or strange with attempting to help people who are visibly lacking the basic necessities of life, and it appears quite reasonable to try to alleviate suffering when this is possible. But to leave a successful position and enter freely, consciously, and intentionally into a position of servanthood seems unhealthy. It is a violation of the most basic human instincts. To try to lift others up to our own privileged position is honorable and perhaps even an expression of generosity, but to attempt to put ourselves in a position of disrepute and to become dependent and vulnerable seems to be a form of masochism that defies the best of our aspirations.

Something of this attitude appears in the expression "helping the less fortunate," which frequently can be heard from the mouths of those who ask or offer aid. This expression has an elitist ring to it because it assumes that *we* have made it and have gotten it together while *they* simply have not been able to keep up with us and need to be helped. It is the attitude which says: "Fate is on our side and not theirs. But since we are Christians we have to lift them up and give them a share of our good fortune. The undeniable fact is that the world is divided between the 'fortunate' and the 'unfortunate' ones. So let us not feel guilty about it, but reach out as good people to those who happen to be on the other side of the fence." In this way of thinking compassion remains part of the competition, and is a far cry from radical servanthood.

Radical servanthood does not make sense unless we introduce a new level of understanding and see it as the way to encounter God himself. To be humble and persecuted cannot be desired unless we can find God in humility and persecution. When we begin to see God himself, the source of all our comfort and consolation, in the center of servanthood, compassion becomes much more than doing good for unfortunate people. Radical servanthood, as the encounter with the compassionate God, takes us beyond the distinctions between wealth and poverty, success and failure, fortune and bad luck. Radical servanthood is not an enterprise in which we try to surround ourselves with as much misery as possible, but a joyful way of life in which our eyes are opened to the vision of the true God who chose the way of servanthood to make himself known. The poor are called blessed not because poverty is good, but because theirs is the kingdom of heaven; the mourners are called blessed not because mourning is good, but because they shall be comforted.

Here we are touching the profound spiritual truth that service is an expression of the search for God and not just of the desire to bring about individual or social change. This is open to all sorts of misunderstanding, but its truth is confirmed in the lives of those for whom service is a constant and uninterrupted concern. As long as the help we offer to others is motivated primarily by the changes we may accomplish, our service cannot last long. When results do not appear, when success is absent, when we are no longer liked or praised for what we do, we lose the strength and motivation to continue. When we see nothing but sad, poor, sick, or miserable people who, even after our many attempts to offer help, remain sad, poor, sick, and miserable, then the only reasonable response is to move away in order to prevent ourselves from becoming cynical or depressed. Radical servanthood challenges us, while attempting persistently to overcome poverty, hunger, illness, and any other form of human misery, to reveal the gentle presence of our compassionate God in the midst of our broken world.

JOYFUL SERVANTS

Joy and gratitude are the qualities of the heart by which we recognize those who are committed to a life of service in the path of Jesus Christ. We see this in families where parents and children are attentive to one another's needs and spend time together despite many outside pressures. We see it in those who always have room for a stranger, an extra plate for a visitor, time for someone in need. We see it in the students who work with the elderly, and in the many men and women who offer money, time, and energy for those who are hungry, in prison, sick, or dying. We see it in the sisters who work with the poorest of the poor. Wherever we see real service we also see joy, because in the midst of service a divine presence becomes visible and a gift is offered. Therefore, those who serve as followers of Jesus discover that they are receiving more than they are giving. Just as a mother does not need to be rewarded for the attention she pays to her child, because her child is her joy, so those who serve their neighbor will find their reward in the people whom they serve.

The joy of those who follow their Lord on his self-emptying and humbling way shows that what they seek is not misery and pain but the God whose compassion they have felt in their own lives. Their eyes do not focus on poverty and misery, but on the face of the loving God.

This joy can rightly be seen as an anticipation of the full manifestation of God's love. The hymn of Christ, therefore, does not end with the words about his downward road. Christ emptied and humbled himself:

> But God raised him high
> and gave him a name
> which is above all other names
> so that all beings
> in the heavens, on earth and in the underworld,
> should bend the knee at the name of Jesus
> and that every tongue should acclaim
> Jesus Christ as Lord,
> to the glory of God the Father.
>
> (Ph 2:9–11)

Without these final sentences we would never be able to grasp the fullness of God's compassion. God's compassion as revealed in Christ does not end in suffering but in glory. The servanthood of Christ is indeed a divine servanthood, a servanthood that finds its fulfillment in the lordship of the risen Christ who received the name that is above all other names. The resurrection of Christ is the final affirmation of his servanthood. And with the servant Christ, all servanthood has been lifted up and sanctified as the manifestation of God's compassion. This is the basis of all our joy and hope: Our life of servanthood is lived in union with the risen Christ, in and through whom we have become children of the compassionate Father. Thus Paul can say, "And if we are children we are heirs as well: heirs of God and coheirs with Christ, sharing his sufferings so as to share his glory. I think that what we suffer in this life can never be compared to the glory, as yet unrevealed, which is waiting for us" (Rm 8:17–18).

3

Obedient God

THE INNER LIFE OF GOD

In Jesus Christ, God reveals himself to us as a God of compassion. This divine compassion is God's being with us as a suffering servant. God is with us, he feels with us deeply and tenderly. He allows our human pain to reverberate in his innermost self. He even goes so far as to give up the privileged position of his divine power and to appear in our midst as a humble servant who offers to wash our wounded and tired feet.

But this is not the whole story of God's compassion. There is an element which we need to explore in depth in order to gain yet another glimpse of the mystery of God's infinite love for us. In Jesus Christ, God did not manifest his compassion simply by becoming a suffering servant, but by becoming a suffering servant in obedience. Obedience gives servanthood its deepest dimension.

Often we experience a strong desire to offer our services to our fellow human beings in need. At times we even dream about giving our lives to the poor and living in solidarity with those who suffer. Sometimes these dreams lead to generous actions, to good and worthwhile projects, and to weeks, months, and even years of dedicated work. But the initiative still remains ours. We decide when we go and when we return; we decide what to do and how to do it; we control the level and intensity of our servanthood. Although much good work gets done in these situations, there is always the creeping danger that even our servanthood is a subtle form of manipulation. Are we really servants when we can become masters again once we think we have done our part or made our contribution? Are we really servants when we can say when, where, and how long we will give of our time and energy? Is service in a far country really an expression of servanthood when we keep enough money in the bank to fly home at any moment?

Jesus came to the "far country" because he was sent. Being sent remained uppermost in his consciousness. He never claimed anything for himself. He was the obedient servant who said and did nothing, absolutely nothing, unless it was said and done in complete obedience to the one who sent him.

We are trying to express here what can barely be put into words: In Jesus, God not only reveals his compassion as servanthood but also as obedience. The one through whom all things came to be, became the obedient one. Karl Barth writes, "It belongs to the inner life of God that there should take place within it obedience . . . in himself he is both One who is obeyed and Another who obeys."[5] In Jesus Christ, this inner side of the nature of God becomes visible. In Jesus Christ, we see that God's compassion can never be separated

from his obedience. Because through Jesus' complete obedience God made his compassionate entry into our broken,
wounded, and painful human condition.

INTIMATE LISTENING

Having said this, however, we must say many other things
to prevent our own distorted feelings about obedience from
interfering with our understanding of Jesus as the obedient
servant. The word *obedience* very often evokes in us many
negative feelings and ideas. We think of someone with power
giving orders to another without it. We think of orders we
follow only because we cannot refuse. We think of doing
things others say are good for us but the value of which we
do not directly see. We think of the great distance between
the one who commands and the one who follows. When we
say, "We do this in obedience," we usually imply that we
have no real insight into what we do but accept the authority
of another regardless of our own desires or needs. Thus the
word *obedience* is often tainted by many feelings of hostility,
resentment, or distance. It nearly always implies that someone is in a position to impose his or her will on others.

None of these negative associations, however, belongs to
the obedience of Jesus Christ. His obedience is hearing
God's loving word and responding to it. The word obedience
is derived from the Latin word *audire*, which means "to
listen." Obedience, as it is embodied in Jesus Christ, is a total
listening, a giving attention with no hesitation or limitation, a
being "all ear." It is an expression of the intimacy that can
exist between two persons. Here the one who obeys knows
without restriction the will of the one who commands and has
only one all-embracing desire: to live out that will.

This intimate listening is expressed beautifully when Jesus
speaks of God as his Father, his beloved Father. When used
by Jesus, the word *obedience* has no association with fear,
but rather is the expression of his most intimate, loving rela-

tionship. It is the relationship with his caring Father who said during his baptism at the river Jordan, "This is my Son, the Beloved" (Mt 3:17), and during his prayer on Mount Tabor, "This is my Son, the Beloved . . . Listen to him" (Mt 17:5). Jesus' actions and words are the obedient response to this love of his Father. We cannot emphasize enough that when Jesus calls God his Father, he speaks about a love that includes and transcends all the love we know. It is the love of a father, but also of a mother, brother, sister, friend, and lover. It is severe yet merciful, jealous yet sharing, prodding yet guiding, challenging yet caring, disinterested yet supportive, selfless yet very intimate. The many kinds of love we have experienced in our various human relationships are fully represented in the love between Jesus and his heavenly Father, but also fully transcended by this same love.

ATTENTIVENESS TO THE FATHER

Thus far, we have primarily used the word *God* to indicate the subject of divine compassion. But it needs to be remembered that Jesus calls this compassionate God *abba*, "beloved Father." Obedience is a listening in love to God, the beloved Father. In this listening there is neither a moment of distance, nor fear, nor hesitation, nor doubt, but only the unconditional, unlimited, and unrestrained love that comes from the Father. Jesus' response to this love is likewise unconditional, unlimited, and unrestrained. We will misunderstand Jesus' going into the world of suffering and pain and his giving himself to us as a servant if we perceive these actions as the heroic initiatives of a son who wants to prove himself to a father whose love has to be earned, or as the anxious fulfillment of a command given by a father whose will must be respected. Rather, we see in these actions a divine listening to a divine love, a loving response to a loving mission, and a free "yes" to a free command.

From the first words Jesus speaks in the Temple, "Did you

not know that I must be busy with my Father's affairs" (Lk
2:49), to his last words on the cross, "Father, into your hands
I commit my spirit" (Lk 23:46), we are made aware that his
first and only concern is to do the will of his Father.
Impressed by Jesus' words and healing acts, we often forget
that his entire ministry was a ministry of obedience. The true
greatness of Jesus' life and words is found in his obedience.
Others have performed miraculous acts, have attracted large
crowds and impressed them with their words, have criticized
the hypocrisy of religious leaders, and have died cruel deaths
to witness to their ideals. If it is men and women of bravery,
heroism, or even generosity that we seek, then many have
spoken words and performed acts at least as remarkable as
those of Jesus. What sets Jesus apart from all other human
beings is his obedience to his heavenly Father. "I can do
nothing by myself . . . my aim is to do not my own will, but
the will of him who sent me" (Jn 5:30). "The words I say to
you I do not speak as from myself: it is the Father, living in
me, who is doing this work" (Jn 14:10). In the moment of his
greatest agony it is to the will of the Father that Jesus clings:
"My Father, if this cup cannot pass by without my drinking
it, your will be done" (Mt 26:42). Jesus' death becomes his
final act of obedience: "He humbled himself and became
obedient unto death" (Ph 2:8 RSV).

It is not surprising that the Apostle Paul considers Jesus'
obedience to be the source of our salvation. To the Christians
of Rome he writes, "As by one man's disobedience many
were made sinners, so by one man's obedience many will be
made righteous" (Rm 5:19). Indeed, just as Jesus' words
gave him divine authority because they were spoken in obedience, so his death made him our divine savior because he
accepted it in obedience.

Thus, the God of compassion is not only a God who serves
but also a God who serves in obedience. Whenever we separate servanthood from obedience, compassion becomes a
form of spiritual stardom. But when we realize that Jesus'

compassion was born of an intimate listening to the unconditional love of the Father, we can understand how servanthood can indeed be the full expression of compassion. Jesus reaches out to the suffering world from the silent center where he stands in full attentiveness to his Father. Mark's gospel presents us with a beautiful example of this movement from intimate listening to compassionate action. There we read, "In the morning, long before dawn, he got up and left the house, and went to a lonely place and prayed there" (Mk 1:35). It is from this place, where Jesus was fully attentive to his beloved Father, that he was called to action. "Everybody is looking for you," his disciples said, and in obedience to his Father he answered, "Let us go elsewhere, to the neighboring country towns, so that I can preach there too, because that is why I came." And he "went all through Galilee, preaching in their synagogues and casting out devils" (Mk 1:37–39).

In Jesus, God's compassion is revealed as suffering with us in obedience. Jesus is not a courageous hero whose act of emptying and humbling himself earns adoration and praise. He is not a super social worker, a super doctor, or a super helper. He is not a great hero who performs acts of self-denial that no one can imitate. Jesus is neither a spiritual giant nor a superstar whose compassion makes us jealous and creates in us the competitive desire to get as far, high, or deep as he did. No, Jesus is the obedient servant who hears the call and desires to respond even when it leads him to pain and suffering. This desire is not to experience pain, but to give his full undivided attention to the voice of his beloved Father.

WITH HIS LOVE IN US

The emphasis on obedience as an essential characteristic of the divine compassion brings a new perspective to our lives. It tells us that following Christ in his compassion does not mean a search for suffering as a goal in itself. Christians have been understandably criticized for having an unhealthy attraction to suffering. But suffering is not the issue. Fellowship with Jesus Christ is not a commitment to suffer as much as possible, but a commitment to listen with him to God's love without fear. It is to obedience—understood as an intimate, fearless listening to God's continuing love—that we are called.

We are often tempted to "explain" suffering in terms of "the will of God." Not only can this evoke anger and frustration, but also it is false. "God's will" is not a label that can be put on unhappy situations. God wants to bring joy not pain, peace not war, healing not suffering. Therefore, instead of declaring anything and everything to be the will of God, we must be willing to ask ourselves where in the midst of our pains and sufferings we can discern the loving presence of God.

When, however, we discover that our obedient listening leads us to our suffering neighbors, we can go to them in the joyful knowledge that love brings us there. We are poor listeners because we are afraid that there is something other than love in God. This is not so strange since we seldom, if ever, experience love without a taint of jealousy, resentment, revenge, or even hatred. Often we see love surrounded by limitations and conditions. We tend to doubt what presents itself to us as love and are always on guard, prepared for disappointments. The skeptic in us does not surrender easily. For this reason we find it hard simply to listen or to obey. But Jesus truly listened and obeyed because only he knew the love of his Father: "Not that anybody has seen the Father, except the one who comes from God: he has seen the Father" (Jn 6:46). "You do not know him, but I know him because I have come from him" (Jn 7:28–29).

There is more, however. Jesus did not come into the world clinging to this intimacy with his Father as if it were his private domain. He came to include us in his divine obedience. He wanted to lead us to the Father so that we could enjoy the same intimacy he did. When we come to recognize that in and through Jesus we are called to be daughters and sons of God and to listen to him, our loving Father, with total trust and surrender, we will also see that we are invited to be no less compassionate than Jesus himself. When obedience becomes our first and only concern, then we too can move into the world with compassion and feel the suffering of the world so deeply that through our compassion we can give new life to others. This is what Jesus himself told us in the astonishing words: "You must believe me when I say that I am in the Father and the Father is in me . . . I tell you most solemnly, whoever believes in me will perform the same works as I do myself, he will perform even greater works, because I am going to the Father. Whatever you ask for in my name I will do, so that the Father may be glorified in the Son" (Jn 14:11–13).

WITH EYES ON GOD

By viewing compassion as an obedient response to our loving Father, we avoid the constant temptation to see it as a noble act of self-sacrifice. This temptation is very great. Many Christians have been plagued by the idea that the more they could suffer, the better it would be. Often Christians have gone so far as to afflict themselves with many forms of pain in the false belief that in so doing they were following the way of Jesus Christ. This self-defeating attitude has led to much criticism. Friedrich Nietzsche is probably the best-known critic in this respect. He writes: "Christianity has sided with all that is weak and base, with all failures; it has made an ideal of whatever contradicts the instincts of the strong life to preserve itself . . . at the bottom of Christianity is the rancour of the sick instinct directed against the healthy, against health itself."[6]

This criticism makes us aware of our tendency to restrict our view of Jesus to his voluntary sacrifice on the cross. We forget that this sacrifice was an obedient response to a loving Father who not only sent his son into the world but also raised him from the dead to sit at his right hand. The "journey into the far country," as Barth calls Jesus' mission, is a journey of love. It is this journey that we are called to join. Each time we make participation in human suffering a final goal, a purpose, or an ideal, we distort our Christian vocation and harm ourselves as well as our fellow human beings. This becomes eminently clear in the lives of the saints and of all deeply committed Christians. Their eyes are not focused on pain, but on the Lord. Their question is not, "How can I suffer most for God?" but, "How can I listen best to him?"

A report about the Korean poet Kim Chi Ha shows how true listening leads to an unrelenting cry for justice and an uncompromising commitment to the search for truth. Repeatedly jailed and tortured by the regime of Park Chung Hee for his eloquent criticism of oppression in South Korea, Kim Chi Ha was sentenced to life imprisonment in 1976. Yet his spirit remains firm and his hope undaunted, for beyond his own suffering and the suffering of his people, he sees the suffering of Jesus Christ. In his play *The Gold-Crowned Jesus*, a leper, the most despised of social outcasts in Korea, encounters Jesus imprisoned in concrete by government, business, and church officials. The leper asks, "What can be done to free you, Jesus, to make you live again so that you can come to us?" and Jesus replied: "My power alone is not enough. People like you must help to liberate me. Those who seek only the comforts, wealth, honor, and power of this world, who wish entry to the kingdom of heaven for themselves only and ignore the poor . . . cannot give me life again. . . . Only those, though very poor and suffering like yourself, who are generous in spirit and seek to help the poor and the wretched can give me life again. You have helped to give me life again. You removed the gold crown from my head and so freed my lips to speak. People like you will be my liberators."[7]

We might be impressed by the great compassion we see in

the lives of witnesses like Kim Chi Ha, but they themselves rarely mention it. They do not enjoy suffering, nor are they attracted to it. They want only to alleviate and diminish it. But they are attracted by the love of God with such power that they perceive suffering and pain as only a part of their vocation, a part they will be able to accept when the time for it comes.

WITHOUT FEAR

In our time, so full of cruel persecution, it is understandable that we ask ourselves if we would be able to undergo the severe suffering we read and hear about. We wonder how to prepare ourselves for it and often concern ourselves with a future into which we project many horrors and tragedies. But if our primary concern were to listen carefully to God in our lives and to discern his will for us here and now, these worries would prove to be unjustified and distracting. Much of our inner restlessness, nervousness, and tension is connected with our worries about the unknown future. Sometimes we try to alleviate these worries by far-reaching plans. But our work for the future should be based not on anxiety, but on a vision of something worthwhile in the present. When our schemes for a new world are only an expression of our unhappiness with the present, we risk engaging in what Thomas Merton called "organized despair."

Obedience is listening to a voice that speaks to us today and allowing ourselves to feel the loving care of God in our present lives. Obedience is giving full attention to what the Father says to us in this very moment and responding lovingly to what we perceive, because God is our loving Father in whom nothing that is not love can be found. Apprehension, fear, and anxiety cannot sustain themselves in his presence. Fear always creates distance and divisions. But in the presence of God fear melts away. "In love there can be no fear, but fear is driven out by perfect love" (1 Jn 4:18).

Thus, when we pay careful attention to the loving pres-

ence of God, the suffering to which we might be led will
never darken our hearts or paralyze our movements. We will
find that we will never be asked to suffer more than we can
bear and never be tested beyond our strength. When we are
led by love instead of driven by fear, we can enter the places
of the greatest darkness and pain and experience in a unique
way the power of God's care. Jesus' final words to Peter are
the strongest affirmation of this truth. After having asked
Peter three times, "Do you love me?" and after having been
assured three times by Peter of his love, Jesus said, "When
you grow old you will stretch out your hands, and somebody else will put a belt around you and take you where you
would rather not go" (Jn 21:18). Although Peter did not
desire it, he was led to the cross as Jesus was. But because it
was love and not fear that led him there, the cross was no
longer a sign of defeat, but a sign of victory.

The reality of this love is shown in the stories of Christians
who have suffered terrible torture in Latin America. A
brother who was arrested and put in prison after working among the poor in Argentina for several years writes:
"What characterized our Christian life during this whole
time in prison was prayer, and more precisely, prayer of in-
tercession. When you hear the despairing screams of your
friends who are in the process of being tortured, and when
you experience your total helplessness to do anything, you
learn that to pray and to intercede with God is the only
worthy human act that one is capable of doing." However,
this letter, which describes a darkness few have experienced,
is filled with a remarkably victorious tone. In the midst of the
darkness, this anonymous brother felt the love of God and
compassion for his brothers in such a new and intense way
that he closed his letter by saying: "It's not easy to find
yourself back in the normal Christian world. It all seems so
shabby, formal, less intense, and less calm. For us in prison the
gospel was our strength, our weapon against evil, against

hate, against oppression." The editor of the *Catholic Worker* who published this letter noted, "The Church in Latin America, and throughout much of the Third World, is being offered a terrible opportunity, which we dare to envy."[8]

This suffering with others in obedience is the way to meet our compassionate God, whose love enables us to live in the midst of the world, serving our brothers and sisters with a deep sense of joy and gratitude.

God is a compassionate God. That is the good news brought to us in and through Jesus Christ. He is God-with-us, who finds nothing human alien and who lives in solidarity with us. He is a servant God who washes our feet and heals our wounds, and he is an obedient God who listens and responds to his divine Father with unlimited love. In fellowship with Jesus Christ, we are called to be compassionate as our Father is compassionate. In and through him, it becomes possible to be effective witnesses to God's compassion and to be signs of hope in the midst of a despairing world.

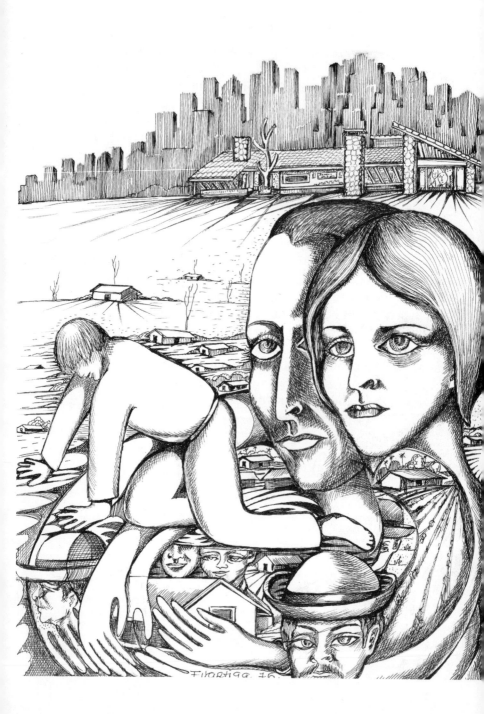

PART TWO

The Compassionate Life

4

Community

NO INDIVIDUAL STARDOM

The main question of the second part of our reflections concerns discipleship. There are many ways to formulate this question: "How can we creatively respond to Jesus' call: 'Be compassionate as your father is compassionate'? How can we make God's compassion the basis and source of our lives? Where can God's compassionate presence become visible in our everyday lives? How is it possible for us, broken and sinful human beings, to follow Jesus Christ and thus become manifestations of God's compassion? What does it mean for us to enter into solidarity with our fellow human beings and offer them obedient service?"

The message that comes to us in the New Testament is that

the compassionate life is a life together. Compassion is not an individual character trait, a personal attitude, or a special talent, but a way of living together. When Paul exhorts the Christians of Philippi to live a compassionate life with the mind of Christ, he gives a concrete description of what he means: "There must be no competition among you, no conceit; but everybody is to be self-effacing. Always consider the other person to be better than yourself, so that nobody thinks of his own interests first but everybody thinks of the other people's interest instead" (Ph 2:3–4). Moreover, Paul stresses that the compassionate life is a life in community: "If our life in Christ means anything to you, if love can persuade at all, or the Spirit that we have in common, or any tenderness and sympathy, then be united in your convictions and united in your love, with a common purpose and a common mind" (Ph 2:1–2).

Precisely because we are so inclined to think in terms of individual greatness and personal heroism, it is important for us to reflect carefully on the fact that the compassionate life is community life. We witness to God's compassionate presence in the world by the way we live and work together. Those who were first converted by the Apostles revealed their conversion not by feats of individual stardom but by entering a new life in community: "The faithful all lived together and owned everything in common; they sold their goods and possessions and shared out the proceeds among themselves according to what each one needed. They went *as a body* to the Temple every day but met in their houses for the breaking of bread; they shared their food gladly and generously; they praised God and were looked up to by everyone" (Ac 2:44–47). God's compassion became evident in a radically new way of living, which so amazed and surprised outsiders that they said, "See how they love each other."

A compassionate life is a life in which fellowship with Christ reveals itself in a new fellowship among those who follow him. We tend so often to think of compassion as an individual accomplishment, that we easily lose sight of its essentially communal nature. By entering into fellowship with Jesus Christ, who emptied himself and became as we are and humbled himself by accepting death on the cross, we enter into a new relationship with each other. The new relationship with Christ and the new relationship with each other can never be separated. It is not enough to say that a new relationship with Christ leads to a new relationship with each other. Rather, we must say that the mind of Christ is the mind that gathers us together in community; our life in community is the manifestation of the mind of Christ. As Paul says to the Romans,

Do not model yourselves on the behavior of the world around you, but let your behavior change, modeled by your new mind. This is the only way to discover the will of God and know what is good, what it is that God wants, what is the perfect thing to do.

(Rm 12:2)

WALKING ON THE SAME PATH

To follow Christ means to relate to each other with the mind of Christ; that is, to relate to each other as Christ did to us—in servanthood and humility. Discipleship is walking together on the same path. While still living wholly *in* this world, we have discovered each other as fellow travelers on the same path and have formed a new community. While still subject to the power of the world and still deeply involved in the human struggle, we have become a new people with a new mind, a new way of seeing and hearing, and a new hope because of our common fellowship with Christ. Compassion, then, can never be separated from community. Compassion always reveals itself in community, in a new way of being together. Fellowship with Christ *is* fellowship with our brothers and sisters. This is most powerfully expressed by

Paul when he calls the Christian community the body of Christ.

The presence of Jesus Christ, whose lordship resides in obedient service, manifests itself to us in the life of the Christian community. It is in the Christian community that we can be open and receptive to the suffering of the world and offer it a compassionate response. For where people come together in Christ's name, he is present as the compassionate Lord (see Mt 18:20). Jesus Christ himself is and remains the most radical manifestation of God's compassion.

The idea that God's compassion as it revealed itself in Jesus Christ is represented in time and space by the Christian community raises many difficult questions for us. In our society, compassion has lost its communal context and therefore has often degenerated into its opposite. We only need to examine some of the ways in which human suffering is presented to us today to come to a better understanding of the communal nature of compassion.

BOMBARDING THE SENSES

One of the most tragic events of our time is that we know more than ever before about the pains and sufferings of the world and yet are less and less able to respond to them. Radio, television, and newspapers allow us to follow from day to day—even from hour to hour—what is happening in the world. We hear about armed conflicts and wars, assassinations, earthquakes, droughts and floods, famines and epidemics, concentration camps and torture chambers, and countless other forms of human suffering close to home or far away. Not only do we hear about them but also we are daily presented with pictures of starving babies, dying soldiers, burning houses, flooded villages, and wrecked cars. The news seems to have become an almost ceaseless litany of human suffering. The question is, do these highly sophisticated forms of communication and this increasing amount of information lead to a deeper solidarity and a greater compassion? It is very doubtful.

Can we really expect a compassionate response from the millions of individuals who read the paper during breakfast, listen to the radio on the way to work, and watch television after returning home tired from their work in offices or factories? Can we reasonably expect compassion from the many isolated individuals who are constantly being reminded in the privacy of their homes or cars of the vast extent of human suffering?

There appears to be a general assumption that it is good for people to be exposed to the pain and suffering of the world. Not only do newspapers and news broadcasts seem to act on this assumption but also most organizations whose main concern is to help suffering people. Charitable institutions often send letters describing the miserable conditions in different parts of the world and enclose photographs of people whose humanity is hardly recognizable. In so doing, they hope to motivate the receiver to send money for relief projects.

We might ask, however, whether mass communication directed to millions of people who experience themselves as small, insignificant, powerless individuals does not in fact do more harm than good. When there is no community that can mediate between world needs and personal responses, the burden of the world can only be a crushing burden. When the pains of the world are presented to people who are already overwhelmed by the problems in their small circle of family or friends, how can we hope for a creative response? What we can expect is the opposite of compassion: numbness and anger.

Massive exposure to human misery often leads to psychic numbness. Our minds cannot tolerate being constantly reminded of things which interfere with what we are doing at the moment. When we have to open our store in the morning, go about our business, prepare our classes, or talk to our fellow workers, we cannot be filled with the collective misery of the world. If we let the full content of newscasts enter into our innermost selves, we would become so overwhelmed by the absurdities of existence that we would become paralyzed. If we try to absorb all that is reported by the paper, radio, or television, we would never get any work done. Our continued effectiveness requires a mental filtering system by which we can moderate the impact of the daily news.

But there is more. Exposure to human misery on a mass scale can lead not only to psychic numbness but also to hostility. This might seem strange, but when we look more closely at the human response to disturbing information, we realize that confrontation with human pain often creates anger instead of care, irritation instead of sympathy, and even fury instead of compassion. Human suffering, which comes to us in a way and on a scale that makes identification practically impossible, frequently evokes strong negative feelings. Often, some of the lowest human drives are brought into the open by a confrontation with miserable-looking people. In the most horrendous way, this was the case in the Nazi, Vietnamese, and Chilean concentration camps, where torture and cruelty seemed easier the worse the prisoners looked. When we are no longer able to recognize suffering persons as fellow human beings, their pain evokes more disgust and anger than compassion. It is therefore no wonder that the diary of Anne Frank did more for the understanding of human misery than many of the films showing long lines of hungry faces, dark buildings with ominous chimneys, and heaps of naked, emaciated human corpses. Anne Frank we can understand; piles of human flesh only make us sick.

How can we account for this psychic numbness and anger? Numbness and anger are the reactions of the person who says, "When I can't do anything about it anyhow, why do you bother me with it!" Confronted with human pain and at the same time reminded of our powerlessness, we feel offended to the very core of our being and fall back on our defenses of numbness and anger. If compassion means entering into solidarity with our suffering fellow human beings, then the increasing presentation of human suffering by the news media does not serve to evoke compassion. Those who know most about what goes on in the world—those who devote much attention to newspapers, radio, and television—are not necessarily the most compassionate people.

Responding compassionately to what the media present to us is made even more difficult by its "neutrality." The evening news offers a good example. Whatever the news correspondent announces—war, murder, floods, the weather, and the football scores—is reported with the same ritualized tone of voice and facial expression. Moreover, there is an almost liturgical order to the litany of events: first the great news items about national and international conflicts, then the more homey accidents, then the stock market and the weather, then a short word of "wisdom," and finally something light or funny. All of this is regularly interrupted by smiling people urging us to buy products of dubious necessity. The whole "service" is so distant and aloof that the most obvious response is to invest no more energy in it than in brushing your teeth before going to bed.

Therefore, the question is, how can we see the suffering in our world and be moved to compassion as Jesus was moved when he saw a great crowd of people without food (Mt 14:14)? This question has become very urgent at a time when we see so much and are moved so little.

COMMUNITY AS MEDIATOR

The Christian community mediates between the suffering of the world and our individual responses to this suffering. Since the Christian community is the living presence of the mediating Christ, it enables us to be fully aware of the painful condition of the human family without being paralyzed by this awareness. In the Christian community, we can keep our eyes and ears open to all that happens without being numbed by technological overstimulation or angered by the experience of powerlessness. In the Christian community, we can know about hunger, oppression, torture, and the nuclear threat without giving into a fatalistic resignation and withdrawing into a preoccupation with personal survival. In the Christian community, we can fully recognize the condition of our society without panicking.

This was convincingly illustrated by Joe Marino, an American theology student who traveled to Calcutta to experience living and working among the poor. The Missionary Brothers of Charity offered him hospitality. There, surrounded by indescribable human misery, he discovered the mediating power of community. In his diary he writes:

One night I had a long talk with Brother Jesulão. He told me that if a brother is not able to work with his fellow brothers and live with them peaceably, then he is always asked to leave . . . even if he is an excellent worker among the poor . . . Two nights later I walked with Brother Willy and he said that to live with his fellow brothers is his first priority. He is always challenged to love the brothers. He stated that if he cannot love the brothers with whom he lives, how can he love those in the street.[9]

In the Christian community we gather in the name of Christ and thus experience him in the midst of a suffering world. There our old, weak minds, which are unable fully to perceive the pains of the world, are transformed into the mind of Christ, to whom nothing human is alien. In community, we are no longer a mass of helpless individuals, but are transformed into one people of God. In community, our fears and anger are transformed by God's unconditional love, and we become gentle manifestations of his boundless compassion. In community, our lives become compassionate lives because in the way we live and work together, God's compassion becomes present in the midst of a broken world.

Here the deepest meaning of the compassionate life reveals itself. By our life together, we become participants in the divine compassion. Through this participation, we can take on the yoke and burden of Christ—which is all human pain in every time and place—while realizing that his yoke is easy and his burden light (Mt 11:30).

As long as we depend on our own limited resources, the world will frighten us and we will try to avoid the painful spots. But once we have become participants in God's compassion, we can enter deeply into the most hidden corners of the world and perform the same works Christ did; indeed, we may perform even greater works (Jn 14:12)!

Wherever true Christian community is formed, compassion *happens* in the world. The energy that radiated from the early Christian communities was indeed divine energy that had a transforming influence on all who were touched by it. That same energy continues to show itself wherever people come together in Christ's name and take on his yoke in humbleness and gentleness of heart (Mt 11:29). This is true not only of Benedict and Scholastica and their followers or Francis and Clare and their brothers and sisters, but also whenever men and women let go of their old, anxious ways of thinking and find each other in the mind of Christ.

Since it is in community that God's compassion reveals itself, solidarity, servanthood, and obedience are also the main characteristics of our life together. Solidarity can hardly be an individual accomplishment. It is difficult for us as individuals to enter into the pains and sufferings of our fellow human beings. But in the community gathered in Christ's name, there is an unlimited space into which strangers from different places with very different stories can enter and experience God's compassionate presence. It is a great mystery that compassion often becomes real for people not simply because of the deeds of one hospitable individual, but because of an intangible atmosphere resulting from a common life. Certain parishes, prayer groups, households, homes, houses, convents, or monasteries have a true healing influence that can make both members and their guests feel understood, accepted, cared for, and loved. The kindness of the individual people often seems more a manifestation of this healing environment than the cause of it.

Servanthood too is a quality of the community. Our individual ability to serve is quite limited. We might be able to help a few people for a while, but to respond in servanthood to all people all the time is not a realistic human aspiration. As soon as we speak in terms of *we*, however, the picture changes. As a community we can transcend our individual limitations and become a concrete realization of the self-emptying way of Christ. This communal realization can then find a specific expression in the daily work of the individual members. Some people work well with teenagers, others with the elderly, others with hospital patients, and others with prisoners. As individuals we cannot be everything to everyone, but as a community we can indeed serve a great variety of needs. Moreover, by the constant support and encouragement of the community we find it possible to remain faithful to our commitment to service.

Finally, we must recognize that obedience, as an attentive listening to the Father, is very much a communal vocation. It is precisely by constant prayer and meditation that the community remains alert and open to the needs of the world. Left to ourselves, we might easily begin to idolize our particular form or style of ministry and so turn our service into a personal hobby. But when we come together regularly to listen to the word of God and to celebrate his presence in our midst, we stay alert to his guiding voice and move away from the comfortable places to unknown territories. When we perceive obedience as primarily a characteristic of the community itself, relationships between different members of a community can become much more gentle. We also realize then that together we want to discern God's will for us and make our service a response to his compassionate presence in our midst.

Thus, God's solidarity, servanthood, and obedience, revealed to us in the life of Jesus Christ, are the marks of the compassionate life lived in community. In and through the community they can slowly become a real and integral part of our individual lives.

A SENSE OF BELONGING

At this point, the question arises, "How can we build community? What do we have to do to make community happen?" But perhaps such questions come from an anxious heart and are less practical and helpful than they appear to be. It seems better to raise the more contemplative question, "Where do we see community occurring?" Once we have become sensitive to the reality of community in our midst, we may find it easier to discover the most appropriate starting point for its growth and development. It makes more sense to sow seeds in soil in which we have already seen something grow than to stand around worrying about how to make the soil fertile.

An illustration from the life of the Trappist monk Thomas Merton might be helpful here. One of the most influential social critics of the sixties, Merton read very few newspapers and never watched television or listened to the radio. Nevertheless, his response to the needs of the world was a compassionate one. Merton could listen to the events of his time and in his solitude discern how to be of obedient service to his fellow human beings. What is important here is to realize that Merton's knowledge of the suffering of the world came not from the media but from letters written by friends for whom particular events had personal significance. To these friends a response was possible. When information about human suffering comes to us through a person who can be embraced, it is humanized. Letters bring life back to a human dimension. In Merton's case, letters came from all over the world and from the most diverse groups of people. They came from monasteries and convents on different continents, from young people wondering what to do with their lives, from novelists such as James Baldwin and Evelyn Waugh, from scholars such as Jacques Maritain and Jean Leclercq, from poets and prophets, from religious, nonreligious, and antireligious people, from cardinals and bishops, from Christians and Buddhists, and from many, many poor people whose names will never be known. In these letters, Merton saw the world with its pains and its joys. He was drawn into a real community of living people with real faces, real tears, and real smiles. Once in a while Merton invited some of his friends to the Abbey, and together they prayed, spoke about the pain of the world, and tried to give each other new hope and new strength. These small retreats proved to be highly significant for those who lived a very active and often dangerous life. They were offered strong mutual support. Many people known today for their courage and perseverance found their inspiration in these experiences of community.

This is just one example to illustrate the importance of community in the compassionate life. Letters and retreats are ways of being in community, but there are many other ways. It is important to keep ourselves from thinking about community only in terms of living together in one house, or sharing meals and prayers, or doing projects together. These might well be true expressions of community, but community is a much deeper reality. People who live together do not necessarily live in community, and those who live alone do not necessarily live without it. Physical nearness or distance is secondary. The primary quality of community is a deep sense of being gathered by God. When Francis Xavier traveled alone across many continents to preach the Gospel, he found strength in the sure knowledge that he belonged to a community that supported him with prayer and brotherly care. And many Christians who show great perseverance in hard and lonely tasks find their strength in the deep bond with the community in whose name they do their work.

Here we touch one of the most critical areas of the Christian life today. Many very generous Christians find themselves increasingly tired and dispirited not so much because the work is hard or the success slight, but because they feel isolated, unsupported, and left alone. People who say, "I wonder if anyone cares what I am doing. I wonder if my superior, my friends at home, or the people who sent me ever think about me, ever pray for me, ever consider me part of their lives," are in real spiritual danger. We are able to do many hard things, tolerate many conflicts, overcome many obstacles, and persevere under many pressures, but when we no longer experience ourselves as part of a caring, supporting, praying community, we quickly lose faith. This is because faith in God's compassionate presence can never be separated from experiencing God's presence in the community to which we belong. The crises in the lives of many caring Christians today are closely connected with deep feelings of not belonging. Without a sense of being sent by a caring community, a compassionate life cannot last long and quickly degenerates into a life marked by numbness and anger. This is not simply a psychological observation, but a theological truth, because apart from a vital relationship with a caring community a vital relationship with Christ is not possible.

Now we must look more closely at the dynamics of community life. We will do so by speaking about the two poles of a mature community life in which God's compassion can become visible: displacement and togetherness.

5

Displacement

MOVING FROM THE ORDINARY AND PROPER PLACE

The word *community* generally expresses a certain supportive and nurturing way of living and working together. When someone says, "I miss a sense of community here; something should be done to build a better community," she or he is probably suffering from alienation, loneliness, or lack of mutual support and cooperation. The desire for community is most often a desire for a sense of unity, a feeling of being accepted, and an experience of at-homeness. It is therefore not strange that for quite a few critical observers of the contemporary scene, the word *community* has become associated with sentimentalism, romanticism, and even melancholy.

If we want to reflect on community in the context of compassion, we must go far beyond these spontaneous associations. Community can never be the place where God's obedient servanthood reveals itself if community is understood principally as something warm, soft, homey, comfortable, or protective. When we form community primarily to heal personal wounds, it cannot become the place where we effectively realize solidarity with other people's pains.

The paradox of the Christian community is that people are gathered together in voluntary displacement. The togetherness of those who form a Christian community is a being-gathered-in-displacement. According to Webster's dictionary, displacement means, to move or to shift from the ordinary or proper place. This becomes a telling definition when we realize the extent to which we are preoccupied with adapting ourselves to the prevalent norms and values of our milieu. We want to be ordinary and proper people who live ordinary and proper lives. There is an enormous pressure on us to do what is ordinary and proper—even the attempt to excel is ordinary and proper—and thus find the satisfaction of general acceptance. This is quite understandable since the ordinary and proper behavior that gives shape to an ordinary and proper life offers us the comforting illusion that things are under control and that everything extraordinary and improper can be kept outside the walls of our self-created fortress.

The call to community as we hear it from our Lord is the call to move away from the ordinary and proper places. Leave your father and mother. Let the dead bury the dead. Keep your hand on the plow and do not look back. Sell what you own, give the money to the poor and come follow me (Lk 14:26; 9:60, 62; 18:22). The Gospels confront us with this persistent voice inviting us to move from where it is comfortable, from where we want to stay, from where we feel at home.

Why is this so central? It is central because in voluntary

displacement, we cast off the illusion of "having it together" and thus begin to experience our true condition, which is that we, like everyone else, are pilgrims on the way, sinners in need of grace. Through voluntary displacement, we counteract the tendency to become settled in a false comfort and to forget the fundamentally unsettled position that we share with all people. Voluntary displacement leads us to the existential recognition of our inner brokenness and thus brings us to a deeper solidarity with the brokenness of our fellow human beings. Community, as the place of compassion, therefore always requires displacement. The Greek word for church, *ekklesia*—from *ek* = out, and *kaleo* = call—indicates that as a Christian community we are people who together are called out of our familiar places to unknown territories, out of our ordinary and proper places to the places where people hurt and where we can experience with them our common human brokenness and our common need for healing.

In voluntary displacement community is formed, deepened, and strengthened. In voluntary displacement we discover each other as members of the same human family with whom we can share our joys and sorrows. Each time we want to move back to what is ordinary and proper, each time we yearn to be settled and feel at home, we erect walls between ourselves and others, undermine community, and reduce compassion to the soft part of an essentially competitive life.

FOLLOWING THE DISPLACED LORD

Voluntary displacement as a way of life rather than as a unique event is the mark of discipleship. The Lord, whose compassion we want to manifest in time and place, is indeed the displaced Lord. Paul describes Jesus as the one who voluntarily displaced himself. "His state was divine, yet he did not cling to his equality with God but emptied himself to assume the condition of a slave, and became as we are" (Ph 2:6–7). A greater displacement cannot be conceived. The mystery of the incarnation is that God did not remain in the place that was proper for him but moved to the condition of a suffering human being. God *gave up* his heavenly place and took a humble place among mortal men and women. God displaced himself so that nothing human would be alien to him and he could experience fully the brokenness of our human condition.

In the life of Jesus, we see how this divine displacement becomes visible in a human story. As a child, Jesus is taken to Egypt to protect him against the threats of King Herod. As a boy, he leaves his parents and stays in the Temple to listen to the doctors and ask them questions. As an adult, he goes into the desert for forty days to fast and to be tempted by the demon. During the years of ministry that follow, Jesus continuously moves away from power, success, and popularity in order to remain faithful to his divine call. When the people are excited because of his healing powers, he confronts them with their sins and is not afraid to evoke their anger. When they are so impressed by his ability to give bread that they want to make him their king, he moves away and challenges them to work for the food that gives eternal life. When his disciples ask for a special place in his kingdom, he asks them if they can drink the cup of suffering, and when they hope for a quick victory, he speaks of pain and death. Finally, these displacements lead him to the cross. There, rejected by all and feeling abandoned by God, Jesus becomes the most displaced human being. Thus, Jesus' displacement, which began with his birth in Bethlehem, find its fullest expression in his death on a cross outside the walls of Jerusalem. Paul gives words to this mystery by saying, "Being as we are, he was humbler yet, even to accepting death, death on a cross" (Ph 2:7–8).

Jesus Christ is the displaced Lord in whom God's compassion becomes flesh. In him, we see a life of displacement lived to the fullest. It is in following our displaced Lord that the Christian community is formed.

TO DISAPPEAR AS AN OBJECT OF INTEREST

We must now look more deeply into the way in which displacement becomes a way to compassionate community. At first sight, displacement seems disruptive. Many people who have experienced harsh, cruel displacements can testify that displacement unsettled their family life, destroyed their sense of security, created much anger and resentment, and left them with the feeling that their lives were irreparably harmed. Displaced people, therefore, are not necessarily compassionate people. Many have become fearful, suspicious, and prone to complain. In a world with millions of displaced people, we need to be careful not to romanticize displacement or to make it an easy prescription for people who seek to live compassionate lives.

But we must also say that especially in a world with so many violent and cruel displacements, Jesus' call to voluntary displacement has a very contemporary ring. It is obviously not a call to disruptive behavior, but a call to solidarity with the millions who live disrupted lives.

The paradox of voluntary displacement is that although it seems to separate us from the world—from father, mother, brothers, sisters, family, and friends—we actually find ourselves in deeper union with it. Voluntary displacement leads to compassionate living precisely because it moves us from positions of distinction to positions of sameness, from being in special places to being everywhere. This movement is well described by Thomas Merton. After twenty years of Trappist life, he writes in the preface to the Japanese edition of *The Seven Storey Mountain*, "My monastery . . . is a place in which I disappear from the world as an object of interest in order to be everywhere in it by hiddenness and compassion."[10] To disappear from the world as an object of interest in order to be everywhere in it by hiddenness and compassion is the basic movement of the Christian life. It is the movement that leads to community as well as to compassion. It leads us to see with others what we could not see before, to feel with others what we could not feel before, to hear with others what we could not hear before.

The implications for each of us individually vary according to the specific milieus in which we live and our concrete understandings of God's call for us. The fact that for Thomas Merton voluntary displacement meant leaving his teaching position and entering a Trappist monastery is secondary. For Martin Luther it meant leaving the monastery and speaking out against scandalous clerical practices; for Dietrich Bonhoeffer it meant returning from the United States to Germany and becoming a prisoner of the Nazis; for Simone Weil it meant leaving her middle-class milieu and working in factories as a common laborer; for Martin Luther King, Jr., it meant leaving the "ordinary and proper" place of the blacks and leading protest marches. But for many people it does not even mean physical movement, but a new attitude toward their factual displacement and a faithful perseverance in their unspectacular lives. None of these men and women, whether famous or unknown, desired to abandon the world. They did not want to escape from responsibilities. They did not want to close their eyes to the great pains and problems of their time. They did not want to withdraw into pietism or self-centered introspection. Their sole aim was to disappear as an object of interest—an object of competition and rivalry, an object that can be bought and sold, used or misused, measured, compared, evaluated, and weighed—and thus become real members of the human family by hiddenness and compassion. As long as our primary concern in life is to be interesting and thus worthy of special attention, compassion cannot manifest itself. Therefore, the movement toward compassion always starts by gaining distance from the world that wants to make us objects of interest.

It is worth noting the great role voluntary displacement

has played in the history of Christianity. Benedict went to Subiaco, Francis to the Carceri, Ignatius to Manresa, Charles de Foucauld to the Sahara, John Wesley to the poor districts in England, Mother Teresa to Calcutta, and Dorothy Day to the Bowery. With their followers, they moved from the ordinary and proper places to the places where they could experience and express their compassionate solidarity with those in whom the brokenness of the human condition was most visible. We can indeed say that voluntary displacement stands at the origin of all great religious reforms.

ST. FRANCIS OF ASSISI

The most inspiring and challenging example of displacement is St. Francis of Assisi. In 1209, this son of a wealthy merchant tore his clothes from his body and walked away from his family and friends to live a life of abject poverty. By moving naked out of the fortified city with its power and security and by living in caves and in the open fields, Francis called attention to the basic poverty of humanity. He revealed not only his own nakedness but also the nakedness of all people before God. From this displaced position, Francis could live a compassionate life; he was no longer blinded by apparent differences between people and could recognize them all as brothers and sisters who needed God's grace as much as he did. G. K. Chesterton writes:

What gave him extraordinary personal power was this; that from the Pope to the beggar, from the Sultan of Syria in his pavilion to the ragged robbers crawling out of the wood, there was never a man who looked into those brown burning eyes without being certain that Francis Bernardone was really interested in *him*, in his own inner individual life from the cradle to the grave; that he himself was being valued and taken seriously, and not merely added to the spoils of some social policy or the names in some clerical document . . . He treated the whole mob of men as a mob of Kings.[11]

In the small group of brothers who followed Francis in his

poverty, the compassionate life was lived. These men, who had nothing to share but their poverty and who made themselves fully dependent on God's grace, formed a genuine fellowship of the weak in which they could live together in compassion and extend their compassion to all whom they met on the road. Their communal life of poverty prepared them for unlimited compassion. Chesterton writes that Francis' argument for poverty was "that the dedicated man might go anywhere among any kind of men, even the worst kind of men, so long as there was nothing by which they could hold him. If he had any ties or needs like ordinary men, he would become like ordinary men."[12]

St. Francis offers us an impressive example of displacement that leads to community and compassion. By moving away from their "ordinary and proper places," St. Francis and his followers illuminated the oneness of the human race. They did this not only by the way they lived together but also by the way they created space for others in their common life.

The history of the Franciscan brotherhood, however, also illustrates that as soon as success and wealth seduce people back to their ordinary and proper places, community as well as compassion is hard to find. This was not only true for the Franciscans but also for many other religious groups as well. It is therefore understandable that the history of Christianity is filled with reformers who constantly displace themselves to remind us of our great vocation to a compassionate life.

If we really want to be compassionate people, it is urgent that we reclaim this great tradition of displacement. As long as our houses, parishes, convents, and monasteries are only ordinary and proper places, they will only awaken ordinary and proper responses and nothing will happen. As long as religious people are well dressed, well fed, and well cared for, words about being in solidarity with the poor will remain pious words more likely to evoke good feelings than creative actions. As long as we are only doing well what others are doing better and more efficiently, we can hardly expect to be considered the salt of the earth or the light of the world. In short, as long as we avoid displacement, we will miss the compassionate life to which our Lord calls us.

Those who, like St. Francis, have followed the Lord faithfully have shown us that by disappearing from the world as objects of interest we can be everywhere in it by hiddenness and compassion. Living in the world as objects of interest alienates us from it. Living in the world by hiddenness and compassion unites us with it because it allows us to discover the world in the center of our being. It is not hard to notice that those who are very involved in the world are often out of touch with its deepest struggles and pains, while those who live in solitude and community often have a great knowledge of the significant events of their time and a great sensitivity to the people who are subject to these events.

Thus, displacement makes it possible to be *in* the world without being *of* it. For this Jesus prayed on the evening of his death: "Father . . . I am not asking you to remove them from the world, but to protect them from the evil one. . . . As you sent me into the world, I have sent them into the world" (Jn 17:15, 18).

SOMETHING TO RECOGNIZE

Let us not mistake the idea of voluntary displacement as an invitation to dramatic action. We might think that in order to become compassionate people we must make great farewell gestures to our families, friends, homes, and jobs. Such an interpretation of the call to displacement is more in the spirit of the American pioneers than in the spirit of the disciples of Christ. What we need to understand above all else is that voluntary displacement can only be an expression of discipleship when it is a response to a call—or, to say the same thing, when it is an act of obedience.

Christians whose lives are marked by impressive forms of displacement explain their movements not as self-initiated projects with clear-cut objectives and goals, but as responses to a divine invitation that usually requires a long time to be heard and understood. St. Francis' dramatic gesture of stripping himself and returning his clothes to his father can only be seen as an act of discipleship because it was the climax of many years of inner struggle to discover God's will. Only very slowly after dreams, visions, and years of prayer and consultation did Francis become aware that God was calling him to a life of total poverty. Mother Teresa tells a similar story. She did not leave her community to work with the dying in Calcutta simply because she considered this a good idea or a necessary task, but because she heard God calling her and she found this call confirmed by those from whom she asked advice and guidance. Those who practice voluntary displacement as a method or technique to form new community, and thus to become compassionate, will soon find themselves entangled in their own complex motivations and involved in many conflicts and much confusion.

This is an important consideration, especially in a time when so many forms of self-styled "holiness" are being promulgated. Even the desire to be a saintly person has become subject to false and often destructive forms of ascetical behavior, a fact that reveals more about our needs than about God's call. Saints and "outstanding" Christians should, therefore, never be perceived as people whose concrete behavior must be imitated. Rather, we should see in them living reminders that God calls every human being in a unique way and asks each of us to become attentive to his voice in our own unique lives.

What does this mean for us in terms of voluntary displacement? If voluntary displacement is such a central theme in the life of Christ and his followers, must we not begin by displacing ourselves? Probably not. Rather, we must begin to identify in our own lives where displacement is already occurring. We may be dreaming of great acts of displacement while failing to notice in the displacements of our own lives the first indications of God's presence.

We do not have to look very long or far to find displacements in our lives. Most of us have experienced painful physical displacements. We have moved from one country to another, from West to East, from North to South, from a small town to a large city, from a small, intimate high school to a large, impersonal university, from a playful work milieu to a competitive position; in short, from familiar to very unfamiliar surroundings. Beyond these physical displacements, our lives may be marked by deep inner displacements. As the years go by, familiar images and ideas are often pushed out of place. Ways of thinking, which for many years helped us to understand our world, come under criticism and are called old-fashioned or conservative. Rituals and customs that played central roles in the years of our growth and development are suddenly no longer appreciated by our children or neighbors. Family traditions and church celebrations that have given us our most precious memories are suddenly abandoned and even laughed at as sentimental, magical, or superstitious. More than physical displacements, these inner mental and emotional displacements threaten us and give us feelings of being lost or left alone.

In our modern society with its increasing mobility and pluriformity, we have become the subjects and often the victims of so many displacements that it is very hard to keep a sense of rootedness, and we are constantly tempted to become bitter and resentful. Our first and often most difficult task, therefore, is to allow these actual displacements to become places where we can hear God's call. It often seems easier to initiate a displacement that we ourselves can control than freely to accept and affirm a displacement that is totally out of our hands. The main question is, "How can I come to understand and experience God's caring actions in the concrete situation in which I find myself?" This question is difficult because it requires a careful look at the often painful events and experiences of the moment. "Where have I already been asked to leave my father and mother; where have I already been invited to let the dead bury the dead; where am I already challenged to keep my hand on the plow and not look back?" God is always active in our lives. He always calls, he always asks us to take up our crosses and follow him. But do we see, feel, and recognize God's call, or do we keep waiting for that illusory moment when it will really happen? Displacement is not primarily something to do or to accomplish, but something to recognize.

In and through this recognition a conversion can take place, a conversion from involuntary displacement leading to resentment, bitterness, resignation, and apathy, to voluntary displacement that can become an expression of discipleship. We do not have to go after crosses, but we have to take up the crosses that have been ours all along. To follow Jesus, therefore, means first and foremost to discover in our daily lives God's unique vocation for us.

It is through the recognition of our displacement and the willingness to hear in it the first whispers of God's voice that we start forming community and living compassionate lives. Once we begin to experience our actual physical, mental, and emotional displacements as forms of discipleship and start to accept them in obedience, we become less defensive and no longer need to hide our pains and frustrations. Then what seemed a reason for shame and embarrassment becomes instead the basis of community, and what seemed to separate us from others becomes the basis of compassion.

NO ORDINARY CITIZENS

To say that our main task is to discern God's call in the actual displacements of our lives does not imply passive resignation to sad, distressing, or unjust predicaments. On the contrary, it implies that we must look carefully at our situations in order to distinguish between constructive and destructive forces and discover where God is calling us. Careful attention to God's actions in our lives thus leads us to an even greater sensitivity to his call. The more we are able to discern God's voice in the midst of our daily lives, the more we will be able to hear him when he calls us to more drastic forms of displacement. Some of us are indeed called to move away from our cities and live in caves; some of us are indeed called to sell all we have, give it to the poor, and follow Christ in total poverty; some of us are indeed called to move away from our more familiar milieus and live with the sick and the dying; some are indeed called to join nonviolent communities of resistance, to protest loudly against social ills, to share in the misery of prisoners, the isolation of lepers, or the agony of the oppressed; some are even called to undergo torture and violent deaths. But no one will be able to hear or understand these very blessed calls if he or she has not recognized the smaller calls hidden in the hours of a regular day. Not everyone is called in the way St. Francis, Mother Teresa, Martin Luther King, Jr., Cesar Chavez, Dorothy Day, Jean Vanier, Archbishop Romero, and Dom Helder Camera were called. But everyone must live with the deep conviction that God acts in her or his life in an equally unique way. No one should ever think that he or she is just an "ordinary citizen" in the Kingdom of God. As soon as we start taking ourselves and God seriously and allow him to enter into a dialogue with us, we will discover that we also are asked to leave fathers, mothers, brothers, and sisters and follow the crucified Lord in obedience. Quite often we will discover that we are asked to follow our Lord to places we would rather not go. But when we have learned to see him in the small displacements of our daily lives, the greater call will not seem so great after all. We then will find the courage to follow him and be amazed by our freedom to do so.

Thus, voluntary displacement is part of the life of each Christian. It leads away from the ordinary and proper places, whether this is noticed by others or not; it leads to a recognition of each other as fellow travelers on the road, and thus creates community. Finally, voluntary displacement leads to compassion; by bringing us closer to our own brokenness it opens our eyes to our fellow human beings, who seek our consolation and comfort.

6

Togetherness

THE MIRACLE OF WALKING ON THE FLOOR

The Christian community gathers in displacement and in so doing discovers and proclaims a new way of being together. There are many motives that bring people together. People often come together to defend themselves against common dangers or to protect common values. People also come together because of shared likes or dislikes. Hatred as well as fear can create togetherness. After the resurrection of Christ, the disciples were together in a closed room "for fear of the Jews" (Jn 20:19), and the rulers, elders, and scribes came together in Jerusalem because of their shared annoyance with Peter and his followers (Ac 4:5).

The togetherness of the Christian community, however, is not the result of shared anger or anxiety; it grows from a deep sense of being called together to make God's compassion visible in the concreteness of everyday living. In the Acts of the Apostles, we get a glimpse of this new togetherness: "The faithful all *lived together* and owned everything in common . . . Day by day the Lord added to their *community* [literally: their togetherness] those destined to be saved" (Ac 2:44–47). The Christian community is not driven together but drawn together. By leaving the ordinary and proper places and responding to the Lord's call to follow him, people with very different backgrounds discover each other as fellow travelers brought together in common discipleship.

It is important to realize that voluntary displacement is not a goal in itself; it is meaningful only when it gathers us together in a new way. Voluntary displacement, as the Gospel presents it, leads us to understand each other as women and men with similar needs and struggles and to meet each other with an awareness of a common vulnerability. Therefore, no form of displacement is authentic if it does not bring us closer together. If we displace ourselves to be special, unique, or outstanding, we simply exhibit subtle forms of competitiveness that lead not to community but to elitism. Those entering monasteries or leaving their countries do so only in the spirit of the Gospel when this brings them closer to their fellow human beings.

It is remarkable how many people still think of priests, nuns, monks, and hermits as constituting a spiritual elite. They speak of them as people living in another world, having their own mysterious practices, and enjoying a special connection with God. The danger of this way of thinking is that it divides the people of God into "ordinary" Christians and "special" Christians, with the result that voluntary displacement no longer leads to togetherness but to separation. True displacement, however, evokes a deep new awareness of solidarity. The criterion for any form of detachment, any form of "leaving home," is the degree to which it reveals the common ground on which we stand together.

This is well illustrated by an event that took place at a circus in New Haven, Connecticut. After many acts of lion tamers and acrobats, the high-wire artist Philipe Petit entered the arena. This agile little Frenchman was going to ask for a kind of attention quite different from that required by the other artists. His act was not as glamorous as you might have expected. In a very playful way, he walked on a steel wire stretched between two small towers, making it seem more like a dance than a balancing act. He acted as if he were conquering the towers and made people laugh with his easy jumps. But then something unusual took place which revealed his real talent. As the end of his performance, he walked down on a wire strung between the tower and the sandy floor. Since this was extremely difficult, everyone followed his movements with special attention. You could see people biting their nails and exclaiming, "How is it possible? How can he do it?"

Attention as well as tension grew and all kept their eyes on his outstretched arms. Everyone was so engrossed in his act that no one realized that for five seconds Philipe had been walking on the safe floor! Only after he himself looked down to the floor with a puzzled face and then up to the stands with happily surprised eyes did the tension break and everyone explode into roaring applause. That indeed was the real artistic moment, because Philipe, the artist, had been able to make his viewers look with admiration at an act that everyone else could do too: walking on the floor! The great talent of this high-wire artist was not so much that he could evoke admiration for an act nobody could imitate, but that he could make us look with amazement at something we can all do together. Therefore, the applause that Philipe received was not simply an expression of excitement over the special feat of dancing between two towers; it was also an expression of gratitude for the rediscovery of the miracle that we can walk together safely on the floor.

This story illustrates how displacement can create a new togetherness. Philipe Petit had to walk on a steel wire to make us see how special it is that we can walk on the floor. The main effect of his being different was to reveal a deeper level of sameness. If we complain that we are not as capable as this artist and only feel less self-confident because of his feat, we have not understood him; but if we come to recognize through his act that we are all part of the same human family, then his displacement is a real service. The Christians who displace themselves by going to monasteries, foreign lands, or places of great need, do not do such things to be special or praised, but to reveal that what separates us is less important than what unites us. And so displacement is the mysterious way by which a compassionate togetherness is realized.

SEEING EACH OTHER'S UNIQUE GIFTS

This new, noncompetitive togetherness opens our eyes to each other. Here we touch the beauty of the Christian community. When we give up our desires to be outstanding or different, when we let go of our needs to have our own special niches in life, when our main concern is to be the same, and to live out this sameness in solidarity, we are then able to see each other's unique gifts. Gathered together in common vulnerability, we discover how much we have to give each other. The Christian community is the opposite of a highly uniform group of people whose behavior has been toned down to a common denominator and whose originality has been dulled. On the contrary, the Christian community, gathered in common discipleship, is the place where individual gifts can be called forth and put into service for all. It belongs to the essence of this new togetherness that our unique talents are no longer objects of competition but elements of community, no longer qualities that divide but gifts that unite.

When we have discovered that our sense of self does not depend on our differences and that our self-esteem is based on a love much deeper than the praise that can be acquired by unusual performances, we can see our unique talents as gifts for others. Then, too, we will notice that the sharing of our gifts does not diminish our own value as persons but enhances it. In community, the particular talents of the individual members become like the little stones that form a great mosaic. The fact that a little gold, blue, or red piece is part of a splendid mosaic makes it not less but more valuable because it contributes to an image much greater than itself. Thus, our dominant feeling toward each other can shift from jealousy to gratitude. With increasing clarity, we can see the beauty in each other and call it forth so that it may become a part of our total life together.

Both sameness and uniqueness can be affirmed in community. When we unmask the illusion that a person is the difference she or he makes, we can come together on the basis of our common human brokenness and our common need for healing. Then we also can come to the marvelous realization that hidden in the ground on which we walk together are the talents that we can offer to each other. Community, as a new way of being together, leads to the discovery or rediscovery of each other's hidden talents and makes us realize our own unique contribution to the common life.

An old Sufi tale about a watermelon hunter offers a fascinating illustration. Once upon a time there was a man who strayed from his own country into the world known as the Land of the Fools. He soon saw a number of people flying in terror from a field where they had been trying to reap wheat. "There is a monster in that field," they told him. He looked and saw that it was a watermelon. He offered to kill the "monster" for them. When he had cut the melon from its stalk, he took a slice and began to eat it. The people became even more terrified of him than they had been of the water-melon. They drove him away with pitchforks crying: "He will kill us next, unless we get rid of him." It so happened that at another time another man also strayed into the Land of the Fools, and the same thing started to happen to him. But, instead of offering to help them with the "monster" he agreed with the Fools that it must be dangerous, and by tip-toeing away from it with them he gained their confidence. He spent a long time with them in their houses until he could teach them, little by little, the basic facts which would enable them not only to lose their fear of melons, but even to cul-tivate them for themselves.[13]

This beautiful tale about obedient service in solidarity well illustrates how compassionate togetherness does not suppress unique talents but calls them forth to fruitfulness. We often think that service means to give something to others, to tell them how to speak, act, or behave; but now it appears that above all else, real, humble service is helping our neighbors discover that they possess great but often hidden talents that can enable them to do even more for us than we can do for them.

SELF-EMPTYING FOR OTHERS

By revealing the unique gifts of the other, we learn to empty ourselves. Self-emptying does not ask of us to engage our-selves in some form of self-castigation or self-scrutiny, but to pay attention to others in such a way that they begin to rec-ognize their own value.

Paying attention to our fellow human beings is far from easy. We tend to be so insecure about our self-worth and so much in need of affirmation that it is very hard not to ask for attention ourselves. Before we are fully aware of it, we are speaking about ourselves, referring to our experiences, telling our stories, or turning the subject of conversation toward our

own territory. The familiar sentence, "That reminds me of
. . ." is a standard method of shifting attention from the
other to ourselves. To pay attention to others with the desire
to make them the center and to make their interests our own
is a real form of self-emptying, since to be able to receive
others into our intimate inner space we must be empty. That
is why listening is so difficult. It means our moving away
from the center of attention and inviting others into that
space.

From experience we know how healing such an invitation
can be. When someone listens to us with real concentration
and expresses sincere care for our struggles and our pains,
we feel that something very deep is happening to us. Slowly,
fears melt away, tensions dissolve, anxieties retreat, and we
discover that we carry within us something we can trust and
offer as a gift to others. The simple experience of being valuable and important to someone else has a tremendous recrea-
tive power.

If we have been given such an experience, we have received a precious kind of knowledge. We have learned the
true significance of Paul's words, "Always consider the other
person to be better than yourself" (Ph 2:3). This is not an
invitation to false humility or to the denial of our own value,
but it is a call to enter Christ's healing ministry with him.
Every time we pay attention we become emptier, and the
more empty we are the more healing space we can offer.
And the more we see others being healed, the more we will
be able to understand that it is not through us but through
Christ in us that this healing takes place.

Thus, in togetherness we call forth the hidden gifts in each
other and receive them in gratitude as valuable contributions
to our life in community.

One of the most impressive examples of this compassionate
togetherness is a community of handicapped people in Rome.
In this community, founded by Don Franco, handicapped

adults and children live together in extended families and call forth talents in each other which before had remained hidden. The beauty of their togetherness is so visible and so convincing that many "healthy" people have joined those who are paralyzed, mentally retarded, blind, spastic, crippled, or deaf and have discovered with them the great gift of community. In this community, there are few people with self-serving complaints, low self-esteem, or deep depression. Instead, they are people who have discovered each other's distinctive talents and enjoy together the richness of their common life.

This new togetherness is the place of compassion. Where people have entered into the mind of Christ and no longer think of their own interests first, the compassionate Lord manifests himself and offers his healing presence to all who turn to him.

GATHERED BY VOCATION

By ceasing to make our individual differences a basis of competition and by recognizing these differences as potential contributions to a rich life together, we begin to hear the call to community. In and through Christ, people of different ages and life-styles, from different races and classes, with different languages and educations, can join together and witness to God's compassionate presence in our world. There are many common-interest groups, and most of them seem to exist in order to defend or protect something. Although these groups often fulfill important tasks in our society, the Christian community is of a different nature. When we form a Christian community, we come together not because of similar experiences, knowledge, problems, color, or sex, but because we have been called together by the same Lord. Only he enables us to cross the many bridges that separate us; only he allows us to recognize each other as members of the same human family; and only he frees us to pay careful attention to each other. This is why those who are gathered together in community are witnesses to the compassionate Lord. By the way they are able to carry each other's burdens and share each other's joys, they testify to his presence in our world.

Life in community is a response to a vocation. The word *vocation* comes from the Latin *vocare*, which means "to call." God calls us together into one people fashioned in the image of Christ. It is by Christ's vocation that we are gathered. Here we need to distinguish carefully between vocation and career. In a world that puts such emphasis on success, our concern for a career constantly tends to make us deaf to our vocation. When we are seduced into believing that our career is what counts, we can no longer hear the voice that calls us together; we become so preoccupied with our own plans, projects, or promotions that we push everyone away who prevents us from achieving our goals. Career and vocation are not mutually exclusive. In fact, our vocation might require us to pursue a certain career. Many people have become excellent doctors, lawyers, technicians, and scientists in response to God's call heard in the community. Quite often, our vocation becomes visible in a specific job, task, or endeavor. But our vocation can never be reduced to these activities. As soon as we think that our careers *are* our vocation, we are in danger of returning to the ordinary and proper places governed by human competition and of using our talents more to separate ourselves from others than to unite ourselves with them in a common life. A career disconnected from a vocation divides; a career that expresses obedience to our vocation is the concrete way of making our unique talents available to the community. Therefore, it is not our careers, but our vocation, that should guide our lives.

The following story about an American family offers a good insight into the difference between a vocation and a career. John, Mary, and their children enjoyed a very ordinary and proper life in a suburb of Washington, D.C. John was a successful researcher in community development. He gave workshops, taught at the university, and produced regular reports like any other good researcher. Mary was a creative woman. She found time outside her family obligations for pottery and weaving. Their children were open and friendly toward the neighbors. All who knew the family respected them as caring people, good citizens, and committed Christians. Yet, in the midst of all their successes, life seemed to lack a dimension that was difficult to articulate. One evening, when John had come home from a lecture he had just given on community, he suddenly realized that his own family was as alienated as most others. The more he thought about it, the more it struck him that he earned his money by speaking about ideals he himself did not realize. He felt like a preacher proudly speaking about humility, angrily pronouncing peace, and sadly proclaiming joy.

When the contrast between his successful career and his unsuccessful life became too obvious to deny any longer, John and Mary took the courageous step of taking their whole family on a one-year retreat during which they lived with very little money, social security, and "success." And there, away from their ordinary and proper place, they discovered life anew. They saw nature as they never had seen it before; they listened to each other as they had never listened before; they prayed as they had never prayed before; and they wondered why it had taken them so long to see what had always been right before their eyes. In this new situation, they began to hear more clearly the call inviting them to live free from the compulsions of the world, but close to each other and their neighbors, and in continually searching for a deeper understanding of the mysteries of life. Here they discovered their vocation, a vocation which had always been there, but which they had not been able to hear before because of the noisy demands of their successful careers.

One of the most remarkable, and in fact unexpected, results of their "conversion" was that, when their vocation re-emerged and moved to the center of their attention their whole world became transformed. Words such as *family*, *friendship*, and *love* became new words expressing new experiences of living. Research was no longer an aspect of a competitive academic life, but the expression of the ongoing search for meaning. Leadership became service, an argument to convince became an invitation to join, and impressive lectures became compelling challenges. Most of all, their new way of being together uncovered in the heart of many other people deeply hidden desires that were never expressed until they were lived out in the concrete life of this American family. What for many had been conceived as only a romantic dream suddenly became real enough to be a reachable goal, an ideal that could be realized. The compassionate life was no longer a fantasy but a visible reality in the vital community of people who had discovered, through displacement, a new way of being together.

A vocation is not the exclusive privilege of monks, priests, religious sisters, or a few heroic laypersons. God calls everyone who is listening; there is no individual or group for whom God's call is reserved. But to be effective, a call must be heard, and to hear it we must continually discern our vocation amidst the escalating demands of our career.

Thus, we see how voluntary displacement leads to a new togetherness in which we can recognize our sameness in common vulnerability, discover our unique talents as gifts for the upbuilding of the community, and listen to God's call, which continually summons us to a vocation far beyond the aspirations of our career.

PART THREE

The Compassionate Way

7

Patience

A DISCIPLINE THAT UNVEILS

In this third and final part we want to raise the question: Is there a specific compassionate way that can be practiced day in and day out? In our reflections on the compassionate life the emphasis was on discipleship. Here the emphasis is on discipline.

Discipline and discipleship can never be separated. Without discipline discipleship is little more than hero worship or fadism; without discipleship discipline easily becomes a form of emulation or self-assertion. Discipline and discipleship belong together. They strengthen and deepen each other. Yet we have so many associations, negative as well as positive, with the word *discipline* that it is hard to give it the right emphasis when used in connection with discipleship. When we say that children need more discipline, that there is a lack of discipline in schools, and that without self-discipline no one can reach his or her goal, the word *discipline* suggests a rigorous effort to keep oneself or others under control and to acquire efficiency in human behavior. Even when we use the word *discipline* to designate a field of study and practice, we are still speaking primarily about efficiency and control. When we use the word *discipline* to express the way to a compassionate life, however, these associations become very misleading.

Discipline in the Christian life should never be construed as a rigorous method or technique to attain compassion. Compassion is not a skill that we can master by arduous training, years of study, or careful supervision. We cannot get a Master's degree or a Ph.D. in compassion. Compassion is a divine gift and not a result of systematic study or effort. At a time when many programs are designed to help us become more sensitive, perceptive, and receptive, we need to be reminded continuously that compassion is not conquered but given, not the outcome of our hard work but the fruit of God's grace. In the Christian life, discipline is the human effort to unveil what has been covered, to bring to the foreground what has remained hidden, and to put on the lamp stand what has been kept under a basket. It is like raking away the leaves that cover the pathways in the garden of our soul. Discipline enables the revelation of God's divine Spirit in us.

Discipline in the Christian life does indeed require effort, but it is an effort to reveal rather than to conquer. God always calls. To hear his call and allow that call to guide our actions requires discipline in order to prevent ourselves from remaining or becoming spiritually deaf. There are so many voices calling for our attention and so many activities distracting us that a serious effort is necessary if we are to become and remain sensitive to the divine presence in our lives.

When God calls he gives a new name. Abram became Abraham, Jacob became Israel, Saul became Paul, and Simon became Peter. We must search for this new name because the new name reveals the unique vocation given to us by God. Discipline is the effort to avoid deafness and to become sensitive to the sound of the voice that calls us by a new name and invites us to a new life in discipleship.

Often we cling to our old names because our new names, our new identities, may point us in directions we would rather not go. After all, Abraham, Israel, Paul, and Peter did not have easy lives after they became obedient to God's voice. They had many hard roads to travel and many perils to face. Intuitively, we realize that there are advantages to deafness and that the promises of our own voices are often much more convincing than those offered by God. But we also sense that by remaining deaf we will remain strangers to our deepest selves and never realize our true identities. Without discipline, we might never come to know our true names. And that would be the greatest tragedy of our existence. Deaf people become nameless people who have no destination and remain aimless wanderers, unknown to themselves and their fellow travelers.

Discipline, thus understood, is indispensable in the compassionate life. Without discipline, the forces that call us by our old names and pull us into competitive games are too strong to resist. In the day-to-day practice of living we need to be able to do something that will prevent the seed sown in our lives from being suffocated. We need a concrete and specific way that can provide formation, guidance, and practice. We need to know not only about the compassionate life but also about the compassionate way.

ENTERING ACTIVELY INTO THE THICK OF LIFE

What, then, is the compassionate way? The compassionate way is the patient way. Patience is the discipline of compassion. This becomes obvious when we realize that the word *compassion* could be read as *com-patience*. The words *passion* and *patience* both find their roots in the Latin word *pati,* which means "suffering." The compassionate life could be described as a life patiently lived with others. If we then ask about the way of the compassionate life—about the discipline of compassion—patience is the answer. If we cannot be patient, we cannot be com-patient. If we ourselves are unable to suffer, we cannot suffer with others. If we lack the strength to carry the burden of our own lives, we cannot accept the burden of our neighbors. Patience is the hard but fruitful discipline of the disciple of the compassionate Lord.

At first this may sound disappointing. It really sounds like a cop-out. Each time we hear the word *patience,* we tend to cringe. As children, we heard the word used so often in so many different circumstances that it seemed to be the word that was uttered when no one knew what else to say. It usually meant waiting—waiting until Daddy came home, the bus arrived, the waiter brought the food, school ended, the pain decreased, the rain stopped, or the car was fixed. And so the word *patience* became associated with powerlessness, the inability to act, and a general state of passivity and dependence. It is therefore quite understandable that when anyone in authority—our parents, the priest, the minister, the teacher, the boss—said, "Just be patient," we frequently felt belittled and offended. Often, it simply meant that we were not going to be told what was really happening, that we were being kept in a subservient place, and that the only thing expected of us was to wait passively until someone with power decided to move again. It is sad that a deep and rich word like *patience* has such a perverted history in our minds. With such a history, it is difficult not to consider *patience* an oppressive word used by the powerful to keep the powerless under control. In fact, not a few among those in very influential positions have counseled patience simply to avoid necessary changes in church and society.

But true patience is the opposite of a passive waiting in which we let things happen and allow others to make the decisions. Patience means to enter actively into the thick of life and to fully bear the suffering within and around us. Patience is the capacity to see, hear, touch, taste, and smell as fully as possible the inner and outer events of our lives. It is to enter our lives with open eyes, ears, and hands so that we really know what is happening. Patience is an extremely difficult discipline precisely because it counteracts our unreflective impulse to flee or to fight. When we see an accident on the road, something in us pushes the accelerator. When someone approaches a sensitive issue, something in us tries to change the subject. When a shameful memory presents itself, something in us wants to forget it. And if we cannot flee, we fight. We fight the one who challenges our opinions, the people who question our power, and the circumstances that force us to change.

Patience requires us to go beyond the choice between fleeing or fighting. It is the third and the most difficult way. It calls for discipline because it goes against the grain of our impulses. Patience involves staying with it, living it through, listening carefully to what presents itself to us here and now. Patience means stopping on the road when someone in pain needs immediate attention. Patience means overcoming the fear of a controversial subject. It means paying attention to shameful memories and searching for forgiveness without having to forget. It means welcoming sincere criticism and evaluating changing conditions. In short, patience is a willingness to be influenced even when this requires giving up control and entering into unknown territory.

Jesus and the authors of the New Testament have much to say about this active patience. The Greek word for patience is *hypomonē*. The fact that this word is translated in different places by different English terms such as *patience*, *endurance*, *perseverance*, and *fortitude*, already suggests that we are dealing with a very rich biblical concept. When Jesus speaks about patience, he describes it as the discipline by which God's life-giving presence becomes manifest. Patience is the quality of those who are the rich soil in which the seed can produce "its crop a hundredfold." "These are people," Jesus says, "with a noble and generous heart who have heard the word and take it to themselves and yield a harvest through their perseverance (*hypomonē*)" (Lk 8:8, 15).

It becomes evident that Jesus considers this patience to be central in the lives of his followers. "You will be betrayed even by parents and brothers, relations and friends; and some of you will be put to death. You will be hated by all men on account of my name, but not a hair of your head will be lost. Your endurance (*hypomonē*) will win you your lives" (Lk 21:16–19). Jesus wants his followers not to fight or flee but to enter fully into the turmoil of human existence. He even goes so far as to tell his disciples not to prepare if they should have to defend themselves in court. In the midst of their suffering, they will discover the voice of their compassionate Lord who will give them his wisdom. "They . . . will bring you before kings and governors because of my name . . . Keep this carefully in mind: you are not to prepare your defense, because I myself shall give you an eloquence and a wisdom that none of your opponents will be able to resist or contradict" (Lk 21:12–16).

The active, strong, and fruitful patience about which Jesus speaks is repeatedly praised by the apostles Paul, Peter, James, and John as the mark of the true disciple. Paul in particular offers us a deep insight into the power of patience. He exhorts his friend Timothy to be patient and gentle (1 Tm 6:11) and writes to the Christians at Colossae, "You should be clothed in sincere compassion, in kindness and humility, gentleness and patience" (Col 3:12). He does not hesitate to offer himself as an example of patience (2 Tm 3:10) and to see patience as the source of an intimate solidarity between himself and his people, "When we are made to suffer, it is for your consolation and salvation. When, instead, we are comforted, this should be a consolation to you, supporting you in patiently bearing the same sufferings as we bear. And our hope for you is confident, since we know that, sharing our sufferings, you will also share our consolations" (2 Co 1:6–7). For Paul patience is indeed the discipline of the compassionate life. In a glorious and victorious statement he writes to the Christians in Rome that through patience we are living signs of God's compassionate love: ". . . we can boast about our sufferings. These sufferings bring patience, as we know, and patience brings perseverance, and perseverance brings hope, and this hope is not deceptive, because the love of God has been poured into our hearts by the Holy Spirit which has been given us" (Rm 5:3–5).

This conviction that God's compassionate presence becomes manifest through our patience, endurance, perseverance, and fortitude, is the main motivation for the discipline of patience. This is beautifully expressed by James when he says: ". . . remember it is those who had *endurance* [*hypomeinantas*] that we say are the blessed ones. You have heard of the *patience* [*hypomonē*] of Job, and understood the Lord's purpose, realizing that the Lord is kind and compassionate" (Jm 5:10–11). Thus, the New Testament presents the discipline of patience as the way to a life of discipleship which makes us living signs of God's compassionate presence in this world.

LIVING IN THE FULLNESS OF TIME

Patience as an active entering into the thick of life opens us to a new experience of time. Patience makes us realize that the

Christian who has entered into discipleship with Jesus Christ lives not only with a new mind but also in a new time. The discipline of patience is the concentrated effort to let the new time into which we are led by Christ determine our perceptions and decisions. It is this new time that offers the opportunity and the context to be together in a compassionate way.

In order to explore more fully this distinction between old and new time and to gain a deeper appreciation for the importance of the discipline of patience, let us look at our impatient moments. Impatience always has something to do with time. When we are impatient with speakers, we want them to stop speaking or to move on to another subject. When we are impatient with children, we want them to stop crying, asking for ice cream, or running around. When we are impatient with ourselves, we want to change our bad habits, finish a set task, or move ahead faster. Whatever the nature of our impatience, we want to leave the physical or mental state in which we find ourselves and move to another, less uncomfortable place. When we express our impatience, we reveal our desire that things will change as soon as possible: "I wish he would show up soon . . . I have already been waiting here for an hour and the train has still not arrived. . . . There is no end to his sermon. . . . How much longer before we get there?" These expressions betray an inner restlessness that often shows itself in feet tapping under the table, fingers nervously intertwined, or long, drawn-out yawning. Essentially, impatience is experiencing the moment as empty, useless, meaningless. It is wanting to escape from the here and now as soon as possible.

Sometimes our emotions are so totally dominated by impatience that we can no longer give any meaning to the moment. For example, even though we know that our plane is three hours late and that there is nothing urgent to do, we can be so full of gnawing impatience that we cannot read the novel we wanted to read, write the letters we wanted to write, or have the quiet time for prayer for which we longed. Our sole, all-pervasive desire has become to get away from this place and this time. There is no more hope in the moment.

Those who travel much often complain how little work they get done during their many hours in airports, planes, trains, and buses. Their well-intentioned plans to study their documents, prepare their lectures, or think through their problems are often frustrated even when nothing special distracts them. It seems that the overriding climate of the transportation world is so geared to moving away from the here and now that any real concentration demands more energy than we can normally muster. The transportation business is, in fact, a commercialized impatience. Impatient people might be difficult at times, but too much patience would mean the bankruptcy of many companies. People have to keep moving, so much so that reading a book in an airport coffee shop can hardly be tolerated.

What is the basis of this impatience? It is living in clock time. Clock time is that linear time by which our life is measured in abstract units appearing on clocks, watches, and calendars. These measuring units tell us the month, the day, the hour, and the second in which we find ourselves, and decide for us how much longer we have to speak, listen, eat, sing, study, pray, sleep, play, or stay. Our lives are dominated by our clocks and watches. In particular, the tyranny of the one-hour slot is enormous. There are visiting hours, therapeutic hours, and even happy hours. Without being fully aware of it, our most intimate emotions are often influenced by the clock. The big wall clocks in hospitals and airports have caused much inner turmoil and many tears.

Clock time is outer time, time that has a hard, merciless objectivity to it. Clock time leads us to wonder how much longer we have to live and whether "real life" has not already passed us by. Clock time makes us disappointed with today and seems to suggest that maybe tomorrow, next week, or next year *it* will really happen. Clock time keeps saying, "Hurry, hurry, time goes fast, maybe you will miss the real thing! But there is still a chance . . . Hurry to get married, find a job, visit a country, read a book, get a degree . . . Try to take it all in before you run out of time." Clock time always makes us depart. It breeds impatience and prevents any compassionate being together.

But fortunately for most of us, there have been other moments in our lives too, moments with an essentially different quality in which the experience of patience prevails. Perhaps such moments have been rare in our lives, but they belong among those precious memories that can offer hope and courage during restless and tense periods. These patient moments are moments in which we have a very different experience of time. It is the experience of the moment as full, rich, and pregnant. Such an experience makes us want to stay where we are and to take it all in. Somehow we know that in this moment everything is contained: the beginning, the middle, and the end; the past, the present, and the future; the sorrow and the joy; the expectation and the realization; the searching and the finding. These patient moments can differ greatly from one another. They may occur while we are simply sitting at the bedside of a sick person and realize that being together is the most important thing. They may happen while we are working on a regular task and suddenly recognize that it is good simply to be alive and to work. They may take place while we stand in a quiet church and realize unexpectedly that all is present here and now. We remember these and similar moments with great gratitude. We say: "It seemed that time came to a standstill; everything came together and simply was. I will never forget that moment." These moments are not necessarily happy, joyful, or ecstatic. They may be full of sorrow and pain, or marked by agony and struggle. What counts is the experience of fullness, inner importance, and maturation. What counts is the knowledge that in that moment real life touched us. From such moments we do not want to move away; rather, we want to live them to the fullest.

The following situation illustrates how such moments can be experienced as moments of truth. We are together with a few friends. No urgent subjects are discussed, no plans are made, no people outside the circle are topics of conversation. Few words are spoken. We know each other's wounds. We know of the many unresolved conflicts. But there is no fear. We look at each other with gentleness and patience, and then we realize that we are part of a great event, that all that can happen in our life is happening here and now, that this moment holds the full truth, and that it will stay with us wherever we go. We realize that we are bound to our friends with bonds of love and hope which no distance in time or space will break. We see what unity and peace really are, and we feel an inner strength pervading every fiber of our being. And we hear ourselves say, "This is grace."

Patience dispels clock time and reveals a new time, the time of salvation. It is not the time measured by the abstract, objective units of the clock, the watch, or the calendar, but rather the time lived from within and experienced as full time. It is this full time about which Scripture speaks. All the great events of the Gospels occur in the fullness of time. A literal translation from the Greek shows this clearly: When the time for Elizabeth had *become full* she bore her son John (Lk 1:57); When the days for Mary had been *fulfilled*, she bore Jesus (Lk 2:6); When the days of purification had been *made full*, Joseph and Mary brought him to Jerusalem (Lk 2:22). And the real event always happens in this fullness of time. The words *it happened*—in Greek *egeneto*—always announce an event that is not measured by outer time but by the inner time of maturation. In the days of Herod, *it happened* that Zacharias was the priest to serve in the temple (Lk 1:5). On the eighth day, *it happened* that they came together to circumcise John (Lk

1:59). In those days, *it happened* that a decree was issued by Caesar Augustus (Lk 2:1). While they were in Bethlehem, *it happened* that Mary's time was full to have a child (Lk 2:6). These happenings are all announced as moments of grace and salvation. And thus we see that the great event of God's coming is recognized as the event of the fullness of time. Jesus proclaims, The time has come to its *fullness* and the kingdom of God is close at hand (Mk 1:15), and Paul summarizes the great news when he writes to the Christians of Galatia, When the time had come to its *fullness* God sent his Son, born of a woman . . . to enable us to be adopted as sons (Ga 4:4–5).

It is this full time, pregnant with new life, that can be found through the discipline of patience. As long as we are the slaves of the clock and the calendar, our time remains empty and nothing really happens. Thus, we miss the moment of grace and salvation. But when patience prevents us from running from the painful moment in the false hope of finding our treasure elsewhere, we can slowly begin to see that the fullness of time is already here and that salvation is already taking place. Then, too, we can discover that in and through Christ all human events can become divine events in which we discover the compassionate presence of God.

TIME FOR CELEBRATING LIFE WITH OTHERS

Patience is the discipline of compassion because through patience we can live in the fullness of time and invite others to share in it. When we know that God is offering salvation to us, there is ample time to be with others and to celebrate life together.

As long as we remain the victims of clock time, which forces us into the rigid patterns of time slots, we are doomed to be without compassion. When we live by the clock we have no time for each other: We are always on the way to our next appointment and do not notice the person on the side of the road in need of help; we are increasingly concerned about missing something important and perceive human suffering as a disturbing interruption of our plans; we are constantly preoccupied with our free evening, free weekend, or free month and lose the capacity to enjoy the people we live and work with day in and day out. However, if this clock time loses its grip on us and we begin to live in the inner time of God's abundance, then compassion becomes visible. If patience teaches us the natural rhythm of birth and death, growth and decay, light and darkness, and enables us to experience this new time with all our senses, then we discover limitless space for our fellow human beings.

Patience opens us to many different people, all of whom can be invited to taste the fullness of God's presence. Patience opens our hearts to small children and makes us aware that their early years are as important in God's compassionate eyes as the later years of adults. It makes us realize that it is not the length of one's life that counts, but its fullness. Patience opens our hearts to the elderly and prevents us from the clock-time judgment that their most important years have already passed. Patience opens us to the sick and dying and allows us to sense that one minute of really being together can remove the bitterness of a lifetime. Patience helps us to give a moment of rest and joy to the driven young executive and to create some silence for busy young married couples. Patience allows us to take ourselves less seriously and makes us suspicious every time our many altruistic and service-oriented plans put us back on the time line of our clocks, watches, and calendars. Patience makes us loving, caring, gentle, tender, and always grateful for the abundance of God's gifts.

It is not difficult to recognize people who are patient. In their presence, something very deep happens to us. They lift us out of our anxious restlessness and bring us with them into the fullness of God's time. In their presence, we feel how much we are loved, accepted, and cared for. The many things, both large and small, that filled us with anxiety suddenly seem to lose their power over us, and we recognize that all we really longed for is being realized in this one moment of compassion.

Pope John XXIII was such a patient, compassionate person. In his presence, people felt lifted out of the depths of their entanglements and discovered a new horizon which made them let go of their many fears and anxieties. Many farmers, office workers, students, and housekeepers are also such persons. In their own quiet and inconspicuous ways, they let their friends, their children, and their neighbors take part in the fullness of God's time and thus offer them God's gracious compassion.

Patience, thus, is the compassionate way that leads to the compassionate life. It is the discipline of our discipleship. Since patience must be woven into the very fabric of our daily lives, we need now to explore in greater detail how the discipline of patience assumes texture and shape in a life of prayer and action.

8

Prayer

WITH EMPTY HANDS

The discipline of patience is practiced in prayer and action. Prayer and action are integral to the discipline of patience. In this chapter we want to explore how in prayer we suffer through the here and now and find the compassionate God in the center of our lives.

At first sight, it might seem strange to connect prayer with the discipline of patience. But it does not require much reflection to realize that impatience pulls us away from prayer. How often have we said to ourselves, "I'm really too busy to pray," or, "There are so many urgent things to do that I just don't seem to have the opportunity to pray," or, "Every time I think about going to pray something else demands my attention"? In a society that seems to be filled with urgencies and emergencies, prayer appears to be an unnatural form of behavior. Without fully realizing it, we have accepted the idea that "doing things" is more important than prayer and have come to think of prayer as something for times when there is nothing urgent to do. While we might agree verbally, or even intellectually, with someone who stresses the importance of prayer, we have become children of an impatient world to such an extent that our behavior often expresses the view that prayer is a waste of time.

This predicament shows how necessary it is to view prayer as a discipline. Concentrated human effort is necessary because prayer is not our most natural response to the world. Left to our own impulses, we will always want to do something else before we pray. Often, what we want to do seems so unquestionably good—setting up a religious education program, helping with a soup kitchen, listening to people's problems, visiting the sick, planning the liturgy, working with prisoners or mental patients—that it is hard to realize that even these things can be done with impatience and so become signs of our own needs rather than of God's compassion. Therefore, prayer is in many ways the criterion of Christian life. Prayer requires that we stand in God's presence with open hands, naked and vulnerable, proclaiming to ourselves and to others that without God we can do nothing. This is difficult in a climate where the predominant counsel is, "Do your best and God will do the rest." When life is divided into "our best" and "God's rest," we have turned prayer into a last resort to be used only when all our own resources are depleted. Then even the Lord has become the victim of our impatience. Discipleship does not mean to use God when we can no longer function ourselves. On the contrary, it means to recognize that we can do nothing at all, but that God can do everything through us. As disciples, we find not some but all of our strength, hope, courage, and confidence in God. Therefore, prayer must be our first concern.

Let us now look more closely at the practice of prayer. From all we have said, it is clear that prayer is not an effort to make contact with God, to bring him to our side. Prayer, as a discipline that strengthens and deepens discipleship, is the effort to remove everything that might prevent the Spirit of God, given to us by Jesus Christ, from speaking freely to us and in us. The discipline of prayer is the discipline by which we liberate the Spirit of God from entanglement in our impatient impulses. It is the way by which we allow God's Spirit to move where he wants.

IN THE SPIRIT

Until now we have barely mentioned the Holy Spirit. But we cannot speak about prayer without speaking about the Spirit God sends to draw us into the intimacy of his divine life. The Christian life is a spiritual life precisely because it is lived in the Spirit of Christ. This can easily be misunderstood, as when we say to each other, "Let us do this in the spirit of him who was so good to us." The Gospel, however, speaks in much stronger language. The Spirit is the Holy Spirit sent to us by the Father in the name of Jesus (Jn 14:26). This Holy Spirit is the divine life itself by which we become not only brothers and sisters of Christ but also sons and daughters of the Father. This is why Jesus could say: "It is for your own good that I am going because unless I go, the Advocate (the Spirit) will not come to you . . . But when the Spirit of truth comes he will lead you to the complete truth . . . all he tells you will be taken from what is mine. Everything the Father has is mine" (Jn 16:7–15).

Thus, receiving the Holy Spirit is receiving the life of the Father and the Son. This Spirit makes true discipleship possible, a discipleship that involves not only following in the path of Christ but also participating with Christ in his most intimate life with the Father. Paul expresses this powerfully when he writes to the Christians of Galatia, "The proof that you are sons is that God has sent the Spirit of his Son into our hearts: the Spirit that cries 'Abba, Father,' and it is this that makes you a son . . ." (Ga 4:6. Cf. Rm 8:15). Thus, Paul could also say, ". . . I live now not with my own life but with the life of Christ who lives in me" (Ga 2:20).

Spiritual life is life in the Spirit, or more accurately, the life of the Spirit in us. It is this spiritual life that enables us to live with a new mind in a new time. Once we have understood this, the meaning of prayer becomes clear. It is the expression of the life of the Holy Spirit in us. Prayer is not what is done by us, but rather what is done by the Holy Spirit in us. To the Corinthians Paul writes, "No one can say, 'Jesus is Lord' unless he is under the influence of the Holy Spirit" (1 Co 12:3), and to the Romans he says, "The Spirit . . . comes to help us in our weakness. For when we cannot choose words in order to pray properly, the Spirit expresses our plea in a way that could never be put into words, and God who knows everything in our hearts knows perfectly well what he means, and that the pleas of the saints expressed by the Spirit are according to the mind of God" (Rm 8:26–27). Prayer is the work of the Holy Spirit.

This indicates that prayer as a discipline of patience is the human effort to allow the Holy Spirit to do his re-creating work in us. This discipline involves many things. It involves the constant choice not to run from the present moment in the naïve hope that salvation will appear around the next corner. It involves the determination to listen carefully to people and events so as to discern the movements of the Spirit. It involves the ongoing struggle to prevent our minds and hearts from becoming cluttered with the many distractions that clamor for our attention. But above all, it involves the decision to set aside time every day to be alone with God and listen to the Spirit. The discipline of prayer enables us both to discern the presence of God's life-giving Spirit in the midst of our hectic lives and to let that divine Spirit constantly transform our lives. Having become free, through discipline,

to listen patiently to God's Spirit and to follow his divine
movements in us, we come to the awareness that this Spirit
reminds us of all the things Jesus said and did (Jn 14:26,
16:8), teaches us how to pray (Rm 8:26–27), and empowers
us to be witnesses to the ends of the earth (Ac 1:8). Then,
too, we understand that the Spirit assures us of the truth (Rm
9:1), brings us righteousness, peace, and joy (Rm 14:17),
removes all boundaries to hope (Rm 15:13), and makes everything new (Tt 3:5).

The discipline of prayer makes us stop and listen, wait and
look, taste and see, pay attention and be aware. Although this
may sound like advice to be passive, it actually demands
much willpower and motivation. We may consider the discipline of prayer a form of inner displacement. The ordinary
and proper response to our world is to turn on the radio,
open the newspaper, go to another movie, talk to more people, or look impatiently for new attractions and distractions.
To listen patiently to the voice of the Spirit in prayer is a
radical displacement which at first creates unusual discom-
fort. We are so accustomed to our impatient way of life that
we do not expect much from the moment. Every attempt to
"live it through" or to "stay with it" is so contrary to our
usual habits that all our impulses rise up in protest. But when
discipline keeps us faithful, we slowly begin to sense that
something so deep, so mysterious, and so creative is happening here and now that we are drawn toward it—not by our
impulses but by the Holy Spirit. In our inner displacement,
we experience the presence of the compassionate God. Paul
writes to Titus:

But when the kindness and love of God our savior for human-
kind were revealed, it was not because he was concerned with
any righteous actions we might have done ourselves, it was for
no reason except his own compassion that he saved us, by means
of the cleansing water of rebirth and by renewing us with the
Holy Spirit which he has so generously poured over us through
Jesus Christ our savior. He did this so that we should be justified

by his grace, to become heirs looking forward to eternal life. This is doctrine you can rely on.

                                        (Tt 3:4–8)

Prayer reveals to us the Spirit of the compassionate God. As such, it is the discipline that supports discipleship.

AN ALL-EMBRACING INTIMACY

We must now seek a deeper understanding of the way in which prayer, as patiently attending to the inner movements of the Holy Spirit, is a discipline of compassion. What has prayer to do with a compassionate life? Does the compassionate life not demand that we be present to those who suffer; does it not require that we enter into solidarity with the poor, oppressed, and downtrodden; does it not motivate us both to move into the thick of life and to experience the hardships of existence in solidarity with the outcasts? How then can prayer be a discipline of compassion?

Many people tend to associate prayer with separation from others, but real prayer brings us closer to our fellow human beings. Prayer is the first and indispensible discipline of compassion precisely because prayer is also the first expression of human solidarity. Why is this so? Because the Spirit who prays in us is the Spirit by whom all human beings are brought together in unity and community. The Holy Spirit, the Spirit of peace, unity, and reconciliation, constantly reveals himself to us as the power through whom people from the most diverse social, political, economic, racial, and ethnic backgrounds are brought together as sisters and brothers of the same Christ and daughters and sons of the same Father.

To prevent ourselves from slipping into spiritual romanticism or pious sentimentality, we must pay careful attention to the compassionate presence of the Holy Spirit. The intimacy of prayer is the intimacy created by the Holy Spirit who, as the bearer of the new mind and the new time, does not exclude but rather includes our fellow human beings. In the intimacy of prayer, God reveals himself to us as the God who loves all the members of the human family just as personally and uniquely as he loves us. Therefore, a growing intimacy with God deepens our sense of responsibility for others. It evokes in us an always increasing desire to bring the whole world with all its suffering and pains around the divine fire in our heart and to share the revitalizing heat with all who want to come. But it is precisely this desire that requires such deep and strong patience. The painter Vincent van Gogh powerfully expresses the discipline of patient prayer when he writes to his brother Theo:

There may be a great fire in our soul, yet no one ever comes to warm himself at it, and the passers-by only see a wisp of smoke coming through the chimney, and go along their way. Look here, now, what must be done? Must one tend the inner fire, have salt in oneself, wait patiently yet with how much impatience for the hour when somebody will come and sit down near it—maybe to stay? Let him who believes in God wait for the hour that will come sooner or later.[14]

One of the most powerful experiences in a life of compassion is the expansion of our hearts into a world-embracing space of healing from which no one is excluded. When, through discipline, we have overcome the power of our impatient impulses to flee or to fight, to become fearful or angry, we discover a limitless space into which we can welcome all the people of the world. Prayer for others, therefore, cannot be seen as an extraordinary exercise that must be practiced from time to time. Rather, it is the very beat of a compassionate heart. To pray for a friend who is ill, for a student who is depressed, for a teacher who is in conflict; for people in prisons, in hospitals, on battlefields; for those who are victims of injustice, who are hungry, poor, and without shelter; for those who risk their career, their health, and even their life in the struggle for social justice; for leaders of church and state—to pray for all these people is not a futile effort to influence God's will, but a hospitable gesture by which we invite our neighbors into the center of our hearts. To pray for others means to make them part of ourselves. To pray for others means to allow their pains and sufferings, their anxieties and loneliness, their confusion and fears to resound in our innermost selves. To pray, therefore, is to become those for whom we pray, to become the sick child, the fearful mother, the distressed father, the nervous teenager, the angry student, and the frustrated striker. To pray is to enter into a deep inner solidarity with our fellow human beings so that in and through us they can be touched by the healing power of God's Spirit. When, as disciples of Christ, we are able to bear the burdens of our brothers and sisters, to be marked with their wounds, and even be broken by their sins, our prayer becomes their prayer, our cry for mercy becomes their cry. In compassionate prayer, we bring before God those who suffer not merely "over there," not simply "long ago," but here and now in our innermost selves. And so it is in and through us that others are restored; it is in and through us that they receive new light, new hope, and new courage; it is in and through us that God's Spirit touches them with his healing presence.

OUR ENEMIES TOO

Compassionate prayer for our fellow human beings stands in the center of the Christian life. Jesus emphasizes the great power of prayer when he says, "Everything you ask for in prayer you will receive" (Mt 21:22), and the Apostle James echoes these strong words when he writes, "The heartfelt prayer of a good man works very powerfully" (Jm 5:16). Compassionate prayer is a mark of the Christian community. Christians mention one another in their prayers (Rm 1:9, 2 Co 1:11, Ep 6:8, Col 4:3), and in so doing they bring help and even salvation to those for whom they pray (Rm 15:30,

Ph 1:19). But the final test of compassionate prayer goes beyond prayers for fellow Christians, members of the community, friends, and relatives. Jesus says it most unambiguously,
"I say this to you: love your enemies and pray for those who
persecute you" (Mt 5:44); and in the depth of his agony on
the cross, he prays for those who are killing him, "Father,
forgive them; they do not know what they are doing" (Lk
23:34). Here the full significance of the discipline of prayer
becomes visible. Prayer allows us to lead into the center of
our hearts not only those who love us but also those who hate
us. This is possible only when we are willing to make our enemies part of ourselves and thus convert them first of all in
our own hearts.

The first thing we are called to do when we think of
others as our enemies is to pray for them. This is certainly
not easy. It requires discipline to allow those who hate us or
those toward whom we have hostile feelings to come into the
intimate center of our hearts. People who make our lives
difficult and cause us frustration, pain, or even harm, are
least likely to receive a place in our hearts. Yet every time
we overcome this impatience with our opponents and are
willing to listen to the cry of those who persecute us, we
will recognize them as brothers and sisters too. Praying for
our enemies is therefore a real event, the event of reconciliation. It is impossible to lift our enemies up in the presence
of God and at the same time continue to hate them. Seen in
the place of prayer, even the unprincipled dictator and the
vicious torturer can no longer appear as the object of fear,
hatred, and revenge, because when we pray we stand at the
center of the great mystery of Divine Compassion. Prayer
converts the enemy into a friend and is thus the beginning of
a new relationship. There is probably no prayer as powerful
as the prayer for our enemies. But it is also the most difficult
prayer since it is most contrary to our impulses. This explains
why some Saints consider prayer for our enemies the main
criterion of holiness.

As disciples of the compassionate Lord, who took upon himself the condition of a slave and suffered death for our sake (Ph 2:7–8), there are no boundaries to our prayers. Dietrich Bonhoeffer expresses this with powerful simplicity when he writes that to pray for others is to give them "the same right we have received, namely, to stand before Christ and share in his mercy."[15] When we come before God with the needs of the world, the healing love of the Holy Spirit that touches us touches with the same power all those whom we bring before him. Compassionate prayer does not encourage the self-serving individualism that leads us to flee from people or to fight them. On the contrary, by deepening our awareness of our common suffering, prayer draws us closer together in the healing presence of the Holy Spirit.

FAITHFUL TO THE BREAKING OF THE BREAD

As a discipline for living the moment fully and recognizing in it the healing presence of the Holy Spirit, prayer finds its most profound expression in the breaking of the bread. The intimate connection between compassion, prayer, and the breaking of the bread is made clear in the description of the early Christian community: "These remained faithful to the teaching of the apostles, to the brotherhood, to the breaking of bread . . . they shared their food gladly and generously; they praised God and were looked up to by everyone" (Ac 2:42–47). The breaking of the bread stands at the center of the Christian community. In the breaking of bread together, we give the clearest testimony to the communal character of our prayers. Just as discipleship expresses itself above all in a new way of living together, so too the discipline of prayer reveals itself to be first and foremost a communal discipline. It is in the breaking of the bread together that the Holy Spirit, the Spirit sent by Christ and the Father, becomes most tangibly present to the community. The breaking of the bread, therefore, is not a moment in which we try to forget the pains of "real life" and withdraw into a dreamlike ceremony, but the festive articulation of what we perceive as the center of our lives.

When we break bread together, we reveal to each other the real story of Christ's life and our lives in him. Jesus took bread, blessed it, broke it, and gave it to his friends. He did so when he saw a hungry crowd and felt compassion for them (Mt 14:19, 15:36); he did it on the evening before his death when he wanted to say farewell (Mt 26:26); he did so when he made himself known to the two disciples whom he met on the road to Emmaus (Lk 24:30). And ever since his death, Christians have done so in memory of him. Thus, the breaking of the bread is the celebration, the making present, of Christ's story as well as our own. In the taking, blessing, breaking, and giving of the bread, the mystery of Christ's life is expressed in the most succinct way. The Father took his only Son and sent him into the world so that through him the world might be saved (Jn 3:17). At the river Jordan and on Mount Tabor he blessed him with the words, "This is my Son, the Beloved, my favor rests on him . . . listen to him" (Mt 3:17, 17:5). The blessed one was broken on a cross, "pierced through for our faults, crushed for our sins" (Is 53:5). But through his death he gave himself to us as our food, thus fulfilling the words he spoke to his disciples at the last supper, "This is my body which will be given for you" (Lk 22:19).

It is in this life that is taken, blessed, broken, and given that Jesus Christ wants to make us participants. Therefore, while breaking bread with his disciples, he said, "Do this as a memorial of me" (Lk 22:19). When we eat bread and drink wine together in memory of Christ, we become intimately related to his own compassionate life. In fact, we *become* his life and are thus enabled to re-present his life in our time and place. Our compassion becomes a manifestation of God's compassion lived out through all times and in all places. The breaking of the bread connects our broken lives with God's life in Christ and transforms our brokenness into a brokenness that no longer leads to fragmentation but to community and love. Wounds that are the beginning of the process of decay must remain hidden, but wounds that have become gateways to new life can be celebrated as new signs of hope. Precisely for this reason, compassion, suffering together, can be celebrated in communal prayer.

In the breaking of the bread together, we reclaim our own broken condition rather than denying its reality. We become more aware than ever that we are taken, set apart as witnesses for God; that we are blessed by words and acts of grace; and that we are broken, not in revenge or cruelty, but in order to become bread which can be given as food to others. When two, three, ten, a hundred, or a thousand people eat the same bread and drink from the same cup, and so become united with the broken and poured-out life of Christ, they discover that their own lives are part of that one life and thus recognize each other as brothers and sisters.

There are very few places left in our world where our common humanity can be lifted up and celebrated, but each time we come together around the simple signs of bread and wine, we tear down many walls and gain an inkling of God's intentions for the human family. And each time this happens we are called to become more concerned not only about each other's well-being but also about the well-being of all people in our world.

Thus, the breaking of the bread becomes an expression of solidarity with all who suffer, whether they be nearby or far away. This leads not to cliques, but rather opens us up to the whole of humanity. It brings us into contact with people whose bodies and minds have been broken by oppression and torture and whose lives are being destroyed in the prisons of this world. It brings us into touch with men, women, and children whose physical, mental, and spiritual beauty remains invisible due to lack of food and shelter. It brings us into touch with the dying on the streets of Calcutta and the lonely in the high rises of New York City. It brings us into touch with persons such as Sheila Cassidy in England, Mairhead Corrigan and Betty Williams in Northern Ireland, Kim Chi Ha in Korea, Molly Rush in United States, Jean Vanier in France, and many others all over the world whose cries for justice need to be heard.

These connections are indeed "bread connections" which challenge us to work with all our energy for the daily bread of all people. In this way our praying together becomes working together, and the call to break the same bread becomes a call to action.

9

Action

HERE AND NOW

If the emphasis on prayer were an escape from direct engagement with the many needs and pains of our world, then it would not be a real discipline of the compassionate life. Prayer challenges us to be fully aware of the world in which we live and to present it with all its needs and pains to God. It is this compassionate prayer that calls for compassionate action. The disciple is called to follow the Lord not only into the desert and onto the mountain to pray but also into the valley of tears, where help is needed, and onto the cross, where humanity is in agony. Prayer and action, therefore, can never be seen as contradictory or mutually exclusive. Prayer without action grows into powerless pietism, and action without prayer degenerates into questionable manipulation. If prayer leads us into a deeper unity with the compassionate Christ, it will always give rise to concrete acts of service. And if concrete acts of service do indeed lead us to a deeper solidarity with the poor, the hungry, the sick, the dying, and the oppressed, they will always give rise to prayer. In prayer we meet Christ, and in him all human suffering. In service we meet people, and in them the suffering Christ.

The discipline of patience reveals itself not only in the way we pray but also in the way we act. Our actions, like our prayers, must be a manifestation of God's compassionate presence in the midst of our world. Patient actions are actions through which the healing, consoling, comforting, reconciling, and unifying love of God can touch the heart of humanity. They are actions through which the fullness of time can show itself and God's justice and peace can guide our world. They are actions by which good news is brought to the poor, liberty to the prisoners, new sight to the blind, freedom to the oppressed, and God's year of favor is proclaimed (Lk 4:18–19). They are actions that remove the fear, suspicion, and power-hungry competition that cause an escalating arms race, an increasing separation between the wealthy and the poor, and an intensifying cruelty between the powerful and the powerless. They are actions that lead people to listen to each other, speak with each other, and heal each other's wounds. In short, they are actions based on a faith that knows God's presence in our lives and wants this presence to be felt by individuals, communities, societies, and nations.

Patient action is a hard discipline. Often, our lives get so overburdened that it takes every bit of energy to survive the day. Then it becomes hard to value the present moment, and we can only dream about a future time and place where everything will be different. We want to move away from the present moment as quickly as possible and create a new situation in which present pains are absent. But such impatient action prevents us from recognizing the possibilities of the moment and thus easily leads us to an intolerant fanaticism. Action as a discipline of compassion requires the willingness to respond to the very concrete needs of the moment.

THE TEST OF CREDIBILITY

Probably no New Testament writer is as explicit about the importance of concrete acts of service as James. He writes, "Pure, unspoilt religion, in the eyes of God our Father is this: coming to the help of orphans and widows when they need it, and keeping oneself uncontaminated by the world" (Jm 1:27). With considerable irony, James shows to the "twelve tribes of the Dispersion"—i.e., the Jewish Christians scattered all over the Graeco-Roman world—the importance of concrete acts of service.

Take the case, my brothers, of someone who has never done a single good act but claims that he has faith. Will that faith save him? If one of the brothers or one of the sisters is in need of clothes and has not enough food to live on, and one of you says to them, "I wish you well; keep yourself warm and eat plenty," without giving them these bare necessities of life, then what good is that? Faith is like that: if good works do not go with it, it is quite dead.

(Jm 2:14–17)

James even goes so far as to instruct his readers about how to speak to those who think that merely having faith in God is sufficient.

This is the way you talk to people of that kind: "You say you have faith and I have good deeds; I will prove to you that I have faith by showing you my good deeds—now you prove to me that you have faith without any good deeds to show. You believe in the one God—that is creditable enough, but the demons have the same belief, and they tremble with fear. Do realise, you senseless man, that faith without good deeds is useless."

(Jm 2:18–20)

After showing how in the lives of Abraham and Rahab faith and deeds work together, James concludes, "A body dies when it is separated from the spirit, and in the same way faith is dead if it is separated from good deeds" (Jm 2:26).

It is obvious that James does little more than restate in a new context Jesus' emphasis on concrete acts of service. When the disciples of John the Baptist ask Jesus if he is "the one who is to come," Jesus points to his actions, "the blind see again, the lame walk, lepers are cleansed, and the deaf hear, the dead are raised to life, the Good News is proclaimed to the poor" (Lk 7:22–23). His actions are the source of his credibility. The same is true of his disciples. Jesus wants them to be people of action. He leaves little doubt about his opinion, ". . . the one who listens and does nothing is like the man who built his house on soil, with no foundations: as soon as the river bore down on it, it collapsed; and what a ruin that house became!" (Lk 6:49). With great persistence, Jesus stresses that the test of true discipleship lies not in words but in actions: "It is not those who say to me, 'Lord, Lord,' who will enter the kingdom of heaven, but the person who does the will of my Father in heaven" (Mt 7:21–22). Indeed, prayer must yield specific fruits. The final criterion of the value of the Christian life is therefore not prayer but action. In the "wordy" environment of teachers, masters, scribes, and pharisees, Jesus wants his followers to discover for themselves that mere words will not bring them into the kingdom.

What is your opinion? A man had two sons. He went and said to the first, "My boy, you go and work in the vineyard today." He answered, "I will not go," but afterwards thought better of it and went. The man then went and said the same thing to the second who answered, "Certainly, sir," but did not go. Which of the two did the father's will? "The first," they said.

(Mt 21:28–31)

Should there still exist any question in his hearers' minds, Jesus erases the vestiges of doubt when he describes the last judgment, in which concrete acts of compassion are the undeniable sign of "unspoilt religion" (James). Perhaps nowhere else in the New Testament do we find the importance of the discipline of action so clearly presented:

When the Son of Man comes in his glory, escorted by all the angels, then he will take his seat on his throne of glory. All the nations will be assembled before him and he will separate men one from another as the shepherd separates sheep from goats. He will place the sheep on his right hand and the goats on his left. Then the King will say to those on his right hand, "Come, you whom the Father has blessed, take for your heritage the kingdom prepared for you since the foundation of the world. For I was hungry and you gave me food; I was thirsty and you gave me drink; I was a stranger and you made me welcome; naked and you clothed me, sick and you visited me, in prison and you came to see me." Then the virtuous will say to him in reply, "Lord, when did we see you hungry and feed you; or thirsty and give you drink? When did we see you a stranger and make you welcome; naked and clothe you; sick or in prison and go to see you?" And the King will answer, "I tell you solemnly, in so far as you did this to one of the least of these brothers of mine, you did it to me." Next he will say to those on his left hand, "Go away from me, with your curse upon you, to the eternal fire prepared for the devil and his angels. For I was hungry and you never gave me food; I was thirsty and you never gave me anything to drink; I was a stranger and you never made me welcome, naked and you never clothed me, sick and in prison and you never visited me." Then it will be their turn to ask, "Lord, when did we see you hungry and thirsty, a stranger or naked, sick or in prison, and did not come to your help?" Then he will answer, "I tell you solemnly, in so far as you neglected to do this to one of the least of these, you neglected to do it to me." And they will go away to eternal punishment, and the virtuous to eternal life.

(Mt 25:31–46)

This dramatic scene vividly portrays the meaning of the discipline of action. Action with and for those who suffer is the concrete expression of the compassionate life and the final criterion of being a Christian. Such acts do not stand beside the moments of prayer and worship but are themselves such moments. Why? Because Jesus Christ, who did not cling to his divinity, but became as we are, can be found where there are hungry, thirsty, alienated, naked, sick, and imprisoned people. Precisely when we live in an ongoing conversation with Christ and allow his Spirit to guide our lives, we will recognize him in the poor, the oppressed, and the downtrodden, and will hear his cry and respond to it wherever he reveals himself. Thus, action and prayer are two aspects of the same discipline of patience. Both require that we be present to the suffering world here and now and that we respond to the specific needs of those who make up our world, a world claimed by Jesus Christ as his own. So worship becomes ministry and ministry becomes worship, and all we say or do, ask for or give, becomes a way to the life in which God's compassion can manifest itself.

THE TEMPTATION OF ACTIVISM

The disciples speak of their actions as manifestations of God's active presence. They act not to prove their power, but to show God's power; they act not to redeem people but to reveal God's redemptive grace; they act not to create a new world, but to open hearts and ears to the one who sits on the throne and says, "Now I am making the whole of creation new" (Rv 21:5).

In our society, which equates worth with productivity, patient action is very difficult. We tend to be so concerned with doing something worthwhile, bringing about changes, planning, organizing, structuring, and restructuring that we often seem to forget that it is not we who redeem, but God. To be busy, "where the action is," and "on top of things" often seem to have become goals themselves. We then have forgotten that our vocation is not to give visibility to our powers but to God's compassion.

Action as the way of a compassionate life is a difficult discipline precisely because we are so in need of recognition and acceptance. This need can easily drive us to conform to the expectation that we will offer something "new." In a society that is so keen on new encounters, so eager for new events, and so hungry for new experiences, it is difficult not to be seduced into impatient activism. Often, we are hardly aware of this seduction, especially since what we are doing is so obviously "good and religious." But even setting up a relief program, feeding the hungry, and assisting the sick could be more an expression of our own needs than of God's call.

But let us not be too moralistic about it: We can never claim pure motives, and it is better to act with and for those who suffer than to wait until we have our own needs completely under control. However, it is important to remain critical of our own activist tendencies. When our own needs begin to dominate our actions, long-range service becomes difficult and we soon become exhausted, burned out, and even embittered by our efforts.

The most important resource for counteracting the constant temptation to slip into activism is the knowledge that in Christ everything has been accomplished. This knowledge should be understood not as an intellectual insight, but as an understanding in faith. As long as we continue to act as if the salvation of the world depends on us, we lack the faith by which mountains can be moved. In Christ, human suffering and pain have already been accepted and suffered; in him our broken humanity has been reconciled and led into the intimacy of the relationship between the Father and the Son. Our action, therefore, must be understood as a discipline by which we make visible what has already been accomplished. Such action is based on the faith that we walk on solid ground even when we are surrounded by chaos, confusion, violence, and hatred.

A moving example of this was given by a woman who for many years had lived and worked in Burundi. One day she witnessed a cruel tribal war which destroyed all that she and her co-workers had built up. Many innocent people whom she dearly loved were slaughtered in front of her eyes. Later she was able to say that her knowledge that all this suffering had been accomplished in Christ prevented a mental and emotional breakdown. Her deep understanding of God's saving act enabled her not to leave, but to remain active in the midst of the indescribable misery and to face the real situation with open eyes and open ears. Her actions were not simply an attempt to rebuild and thus to overcome the evils she had seen, but a reminder to her people that God is not a God of hatred and violence but a God of tenderness and compassion. Maybe only those who have suffered much will understand what it means that Christ suffered our pains and accomplished our reconciliation on the cross.

NOT WITHOUT CONFRONTATION

But activism is not the only temptation that requires discipline. Impatient action not only leads to overworked and overcommitted people but also tends to sentimentalize compassion. Therefore, sentimentality is another temptation for which we need the discipline of action. When we are primarily concerned about being liked, accepted, praised, or rewarded, we become very selective in our dos and don'ts. We then tend to limit ourselves to those activities that elicit sympathetic responses. Here we touch on an aspect of compassion that we seldom recognize as such: confrontation. In our society, the discipline of action frequently requires the courage to confront. We are inclined to associate compassion with actions by which wounds are healed and pains relieved. But in a time in which many people can no longer exercise their human rights, millions are hungry, and the whole human race lives under the threat of nuclear holocaust, compassionate action means more than offering help to the suffering. The power of evil has become so blatantly visible in individuals as well as in the social structures that dominate their lives that nothing less than strong and unambiguous confrontation is called for. Compassion does not exclude confrontation. On the contrary, confrontation is an integral part of compassion. Confrontation can indeed be an authentic expression of compassion. The whole prophetic tradition makes this clear, and Jesus is no exception. Sadly enough, Jesus has been presented for so long as a meek and mild person that we seldom realize how differently the Gospels depict him.

In Passolini's film, *The Gospel According to St. Matthew*, we are faced with an aggressive and abrasive prophet who does not avoid irritating people and who at times even seems to invite a negative response. Although Passolini's portrayal of Jesus is one-sided, there is no doubt that he reminds us again of how often Jesus engaged in confrontation and how unconcerned he was about being tactful and pleasing others.

Honest, direct confrontation is a true expression of compassion. As Christians, we are *in* the world without being *of* it. It is precisely this position that renders confrontation both possible and necessary. The illusion of power must be unmasked, idolatry must be undone, oppression and exploitation must be fought, and all who participate in these evils must be confronted. This is compassion. We cannot suffer with the poor when we are unwilling to confront those persons and systems that cause poverty. We cannot set the captives free when we do not want to confront those who carry the keys. We cannot profess our solidarity with those who are oppressed when we are unwilling to confront the oppressor. Compassion without confrontation fades quickly into fruitless sentimental commiseration.

But if confrontation is to be an expression of patient action, it must be humble. Our constant temptation is to fall into self-righteous revenge or self-serving condemnation. The danger here is that our own witness can blind us. When confrontation is tainted by desire for attention, need for revenge, or greed for power, it can easily become self-serving and cease to be compassionate.

It is not easy to confront compassionately. Self-right-eousness always lurks around the corner, and violent anger is a real temptation. Probably the best criterion for determin-ing whether our confrontation is compassionate rather than offensive, and our anger righteous rather than self-righteous, is to ask ourselves if we ourselves can be so confronted. Can we learn from indignation directed at us? When we can be confronted by a NO from others, we will be more able to confront with a NO. Saying NO to evil and destruction in the awareness that they dwell in our own heart is a humble NO. When we say NO with humility, this NO is also a call for our own conversion. No to racial injustice means a call to look our own bigotry straight in the eye, and NO to world hunger calls upon us to recognize our own lack of poverty. No to war requires us to come to terms with our own violence and aggression, and NO to oppression and torture forces us to deal directly with our own insensitivities. And so all our NO's be-come challenges to purify our own hearts.

In this sense, confrontation always includes self-confronta-tion. This self-confrontation prevents us from becoming alienated from the world we confront. Thomas Merton saw this clearly when he wrote:

The world as pure object is something that is not there. It is not a reality outside us for which we exist . . . It is a living and self-creating mystery of which I myself am a part, to which I am myself my own unique door. When I find the world in my own ground, it is impossible to be alienated by it.[16]

Here we find the key to compassionate confrontation. The evil that needs to be confronted and fought has an accom-plice in the human heart, including our own. Therefore, each attempt to confront evil in the world calls for the realization that there are always two fronts on which the struggle takes place: an outer and an inner front. For confrontation to become and remain compassionate, these fronts should never be separated.

IN GRATITUDE

Whether they confront evil in the world or support the good, disciplined actions are always characterized by gratitude. Anger can make us active and can even unleash in us much creative energy. But not for long. The social activists of the 1960s who allowed their anger to fuel their actions soon found themselves burned out. Often they reached a state of physical as well as mental exhaustion and needed psychotherapy or a "new spirituality." To persevere without visible success we need a spirit of gratitude. An angry action is born of the experience of being hurt; a grateful action is born of the experience of healing. Angry actions want to take; grateful actions want to share. Gratitude is the mark of action undertaken as part of the discipline of patience. It is a response to grace. It leads us not to conquer or destroy, but to give visibility to a good that is already present. Therefore, the compassionate life is a grateful life, and actions born out of gratefulness are not compulsive but free, not somber but joyful, not fanatical but liberating. When gratitude is the source of our actions, our giving becomes receiving, and those to whom we minister become our ministers because in the center of our care for others we sense a caring presence, and in the midst of our efforts we sense an encouraging support. When this happens we can remain joyful and peaceful even when there are few successes to brag about.

A beautiful example of this attitude was demonstrated by Cesar Chavez and his staff when they were defeated after a long campaign for Proposition 14, which tried to secure the right of farmworkers to organize. Instead of a sense of depression, there was a party. Instead of a sense of defeat, there was a sense of victory. A puzzled reporter wrote: "If they celebrate with such joyful festivity when they lose, what will it be like when they win?" What became clear was that Cesar Chavez and the many men and women who had joined him in the campaign for Proposition 14 were so convinced of the righteousness of their actions that the final result became secondary to the value of the action itself. There had been long days of praying and fasting to keep the campaign truthful and honest. There had been hours of singing, scripture reading, and breaking bread together to remind each other that the fruits of all actions come from God. And when finally the action failed and the desired result did not come about, people did not lose hope and courage but simply decided to try again next time. Meanwhile, they had experienced a deep community with each other, had come to know many generous people, and had received a keen sense of God's presence in their midst. They felt that there were reasons to celebrate and be grateful. So no one went home defeated. All had a story to tell, the story of the experience of God's compassion when people gather in his name.

Gratitude is indeed a sign of an action guided by the discipline of patience. Even when there are no concrete results, the act itself can still be a revelation of God's caring presence here and now. Such action is true action because it is born of true knowledge of God's active presence. It grows not from the need to prove anything or to persuade anyone, but from the desire to give free witness to that which is profoundly real. We find this most powerfully put into words by St. John:

> Something which has existed since the beginning,
> that we have heard,
> that we have seen with our own eyes;
> that we have watched
> and touched with our hands:
> the Word, who is life—

this is our subject.
That life was made visible:
we saw it and we are giving our testimony,
telling you of the eternal life
which was with the Father and has been made visible to us.
What we have seen and heard
we are telling you
so that you too may be in union with us,
as we are in union
with the Father
and with his Son Jesus Christ.
We are writing this to you to make our own joy complete.

(1 Jn 1:1–4)

These words are a most eloquent formulation of the meaning of compassionate action. It is the free, joyful, and, above all, grateful manifestation of an encounter that has taken place. The enormous energy with which John, Peter, Paul, and all the disciples "conquered" their world with the message of Jesus Christ came from that encounter. They did not have to convince themselves or each other that they were doing a good thing; they had no doubts concerning the value of their work; they had no hesitation about the relevance of their action. They could do nothing other than speak about him, praise him, thank him, and worship him because it was he whom they had heard, seen, and touched. They could do nothing other than bring light to the blind, freedom to the captives, and liberty to the oppressed because there they met him again. They could do nothing other than call people together into a new fellowship because thus he would be in their midst. Since Jesus Christ had become their true life, their true concern, their true compassion, and their true love, living became acting and all of life became an ongoing expression of thanks for God's great gift of himself.

This is the deepest meaning of compassionate action. It is the grateful, free, and joyful expression of the great encoun-

ter with the compassionate God. And it will be fruitful even
when we can see neither how nor why. In and through such
action, we realize that indeed all is grace and that our only
possible response is gratitude.

Conclusion

The great news we have received is that God is a compassionate God. In Jesus Christ the obedient servant, who did not cling to his divinity but emptied himself and became as we are, God has revealed the fullness of his compassion. He is Immanuel, God-with-us. The great call we have heard is to live a compassionate life. In the community formed in displacement and leading to a new way of being together, we can become disciples—living manifestations of God's presence in this world. The great task we have been given is to walk the compassionate way. Through the discipline of patience, practiced in prayer and action, the life of discipleship becomes real and fruitful.

As long as we live on this earth, our lives as Christians must be marked by compassion. But we must not conclude these reflections on compassion without observing that the compassionate life is not our final goal. In fact, we can only live the compassionate life to the fullest when we know that it points beyond itself. We know that he who emptied and humbled himself has been raised high and has been given a name above all other names, and we know too that he left us to prepare a place for us where suffering will be overcome and compassion no longer necessary. There is a new heaven and a new earth for which we hope with patient expectation. This is the vision presented in the Book of Revelation:

Then I saw a new heaven and a new earth; the first heaven and the first earth had disappeared now, and there was no longer any sea. I saw the holy city, and the new Jerusalem, coming down from God out of heaven, as beautiful as a bride all dressed for her husband. Then I heard a loud voice call from the throne, "You see this city? Here God lives among men. He will make his home among them; they shall be his people, and he will be their God; his name is God-with-them. He will wipe away all tears from their eyes; there will be no more death, and no more mourning or sadness. The world of the past has gone."

(Rv 21: 1–4)

This is the vision that guides us. This vision makes us share one another's burdens, carry our crosses together, and unite for a better world. This vision takes the despair out of death and the morbidity out of suffering, and opens new horizons. This vision also gives us the energy to manifest its first realization in the midst of the complexities of life. This vision is indeed of a future world. But it is no utopia. The future has already begun and is revealed each time strangers are welcomed, the naked are clothed, the sick and prisoners are visited, and oppression is overcome. Through these grateful actions the first glimpses of a new heaven and a new earth can be seen.

In the new city, God will live among us, but each time two or three gather in the name of Jesus he is already in our midst. In the new city, all tears will be wiped away, but each time people eat bread and drink wine in his memory, smiles appear on strained faces. In the new city, the whole creation will be made new, but each time prison walls are broken down, poverty is dispelled, and wounds are carefully attended, the old earth is already giving way to the new. Through compassionate action, the old is not just old anymore and pain not just pain any longer. Although we are still waiting in expectation, the first signs of the new earth and the new heaven, which have been promised to us and for which we hope, are already visible in the community of faith where the compassionate God reveals himself. This is the foundation of our faith, the basis of our hope, and the source of our love.

Epilogue

The drawings in this book may prove to be more important than the words. Therefore, we will not close this book without telling the painful story that gave birth to these drawings.

One question kept haunting us as we wrote: Are we, well-fed, well-dressed, well-housed, and well-protected people, the ones who should write about compassion? Can we claim that we know to any degree what suffering is, and can we honestly enter into solidarity with those whose lives are literally broken? Although we tried not to become paralyzed by guilt feelings but instead attempted to explore as sincerely as possible our own limited spiritual territories, we still remained painfully aware of the agonizing cries of the millions of people burdened by cruel oppression. As we worked on this book, we read about families dying of hunger and cold, we heard about the systematic killing of indigenous tribes, we were confronted day after day with the imprisonment and torture of men, women, and even children all over the world. Sometimes this knowledge entered so deeply into our hearts that we were tempted to give up writing and to hide ourselves with tears of shame. However, we kept resisting this temptation in the hope that our writing would be an expression not of hypocrisy but of a sincere desire to participate in the confrontation and eradication of the enormous injustices in our world.

In the midst of all these self-doubts and hesitations, a man emerged from the hazy background of our ambiguous feelings and presented himself to us as a representative of the world that seemed to accuse us. His name is Joel Filártiga, a medical doctor living and working with the poorest of the poor in Paraguay. With his wife, Nidia, and the help of his children, he runs a small clinic in Ybyqui, a town two hours' drive from the capital, Asunción. There people come from great distances, walking or riding in little horse-drawn carts, to ask help for their many illnesses. Joel understands his people. He not only knows the illnesses of their bodies but also feels deeply the afflictions in their souls. He speaks their language, Guarani, and listens to the stories of their long struggles, and suffers in his heart with them. While he listens to their souls cry out, he picks up his pencil and draws, draws, draws. From his hands have appeared shockingly powerful drawings in which the agony of the people of Paraguay is expressed and lifted up in an indignant protest. Through his art, Joel Filártiga has become one of the most outspoken defenders of the poor, and one of the sharpest critics of the oppressive Stroessner regime. Through his art he has become much more than a very capable country doctor. He has become a man who, with his pens and pencils, can shout far beyond the boundaries of his country and plead for understanding and support.

The more we heard about Joel, the more we began to realize what compassion is. It is hard work; it is crying out with those in pain; it is tending the wounds of the poor and caring for their lives; it is defending the weak and indignantly accusing those who violate their humanity; it is joining with the oppressed in their struggle for justice; it is pleading for help, with all possible means, from any person who has ears to hear and eyes to see. In short, it is a willingness to lay down our lives for our friends.

Not long after Joel Filártiga became known to us, we learned the price he had to pay for his compassion. On March 30, 1976, the police kidnapped his seventeen-year-old son, Joelito, and within a few hours, tortured him to death. Those who had been unable to kill the popular and dearly loved father did not hesitate to take revenge by the brutal murder of his teenage son. Joel's and Nidia's grief and mourning did not drive them into silence and seclusion. Instead, they cried out in acts of fearless protest, doing so at the risk of their own lives. Instead of dressing their son's electroshocked, burned, and distorted body in fine clothes and making it look peaceful, they laid it naked on the bloody mattress on which it had been found. Thus, the hundreds of people who came to offer condolences were confronted with the evil attempt to silence a compassionate voice, and were reminded of Jesus' words, "Because you do not belong to the world . . . the world hates you" (Jn 15:19).

In August, a few months after Joelito's death, one of us visited Joel Filártiga in Paraguay and asked him to take part in our efforts to express for our time the meaning of Jesus' call to compassion. We felt that this man knew and could help us to know. In the midst of his grief for Joelito, Joel found comfort and consolation in the drawings he made for this book. He drew during the long nights when deep sorrow kept him awake. He drew after long, anxious sessions with judges and lawyers to ask for justice, and he drew after hours of tears. But he drew with hope—hope for himself, his family, his patients, and his people. He drew so that many should know and be converted. He drew so that his dearly-bought compassion would not be quenched but would become a fire that warms the hearts of many to work and pray for justice and peace. It is because of people such as Joel that this book is worth publishing. Therefore, we have dedicated this book to him and to his wife in memory of their beloved son Joelito.

Notes

1. Worsthorne, Peregrine. "A Universe of Hospital Patients. Further Remarks on the British Condition," *Harpers* 251, November 1975, p. 38.

2. Barth, Karl. *Church Dogmatics*, IV/1 (Edinburgh: T. & T. Clark, Sons, 1956), p. 190.

3. Ibid., p. 188.

4. Ibid., p. 191.

5. Ibid., p. 201.

6. Nietzsche, Friedrich. "The Anti-Christ," secs. 5, 51, in *The Portable Nietzsche*, edited and translated by Walter Kaufmann (New York: The Viking Press, 1954).

7. Cited in Chong Sun Kim and Shelly Killen, "Open the Prison Gates and Set My Soul Free," *Sojourners*, April 1979, p. 15.

8. *Catholic Worker*, Vol. XLII, No. 7, September 1977.

9. Marino, Joe. Unpublished diary written in Rome, May 1978.

10. Merton, Thomas. Preface to the Japanese edition of *The Seven Storey Mountain* (*Nanae No Yama*) (Tokyo: Toyo Publishing Company, 1965). Trans. by Kudo Takishi.

11. Chesterton, Gilbert K. *St. Francis of Assisi* (Garden City: Doubleday Image Books, 1957), pp. 96–97.

12. Ibid., p. 101.

13. Shah, Indries. *The Way of the Sufi* (New York: E. P. Dutton & Co., Inc., 1970), p. 207 ff.

14. *The Complete Letters of Vincent van Gogh* (Greenwich, Conn.: New York Graphic Society), Vol. I, p. 197.

15. Bonhoeffer, Dietrich. *Life Together* (New York: Harpers, 1954), p. 86.

16. Merton, Thomas. *Contemplation in a World of Action* (Garden City: Doubleday Image Books, 1971), pp. 154–55.

ABOUT THE AUTHORS

Donald P. McNeill, a priest in the Congregation of Holy Cross, is presently teaching at the University of Notre Dame, and is the director of the Center for Experiential Learning there.

Douglas A. Morrison, a priest of the archdiocese of Hartford, Connecticut, is presently teaching at Catholic University in Washington, D.C., and is the director of The Pastoral Center there.

Henri J. M. Nouwen, a priest of the archdiocese of Utrecht, the Netherlands, taught at Yale Divinity School for ten years and is presently living as a family brother at the Abbey of the Genesee in upstate New York.

Joel Filártiga, a medical doctor in Paraguay, drew the illustrations for this book in memory of his seventeen-year-old son, Joelito, who was tortured to death by a police squad in 1976.